Religion and human experience

Opposing Viewpoints

Religion and human experience
Opposing Viewpoints

David L. Bender
Bruno Leone

OPPOSING VIEWPOINTS SERIES

Greenhaven Press

**577 SHOREVIEW PARK ROAD
ST. PAUL, MINNESOTA 55112**

© Copyright 1981 by Greenhaven Press, Inc.

ISBN 0-89908-308-0 Paper Edition
ISBN 0-89908-333-1 Library Edition

CONGRESS SHALL MAKE NO LAW... ABRIDGING THE FREEDOM OF SPEECH, OR OF THE PRESS

first amendment to the U.S. Constitution

The basic foundation of our democracy is the first amendment guarantee of freedom of expression. The OPPOSING VIEWPOINTS SERIES is dedicated to the concept of this basic freedom and the idea that it is more important to practice it than to enshrine it.

TABLE OF CONTENTS   Page

the Opposing viewpoints series

THE IMPORTANCE OF EXAMINING OPPOSING VIEWPOINTS

The purpose of this book, and the Opposing Viewpoints Series as a whole, is to confront you with alternative points of view on complex and sensitive issues.

Perhaps the best way to inform yourself is to analyze the positions of those who are regarded as experts and well studied on the issues. It is important to consider every variety of opinion in an attempt to determine the truth. Opinions from the mainstream of society should be examined. Also important are opinions that are considered radical, reactionary, minority or stigmatized by some other uncomplimentary label. An important lesson of history is the fact that many unpopular and even despised opinions eventually gained widespread acceptance. The opinions of Socrates, Jesus and Galileo are good examples of this.

You will approach this book with opinions of your own on the issues debated within it. To have a good grasp of your own viewpoint you must understand the arguments of those with whom you disagree. It is said that those who do not completely understand their adversary's point of view do not fully understand their own.

Perhaps the most persuasive case for considering opposing viewpoints has been presented by John Stuart Mill in his work *On Liberty*. Consider the following statements of his when studying controversial issues.

THE OPINIONS OF OTHERS

If all mankind minus one were of one opinion, and only one person were of the contrary opinion, mankind would be no more justified in silencing that one person than he, if he had the power, would be justified in silencing mankind....

We can never be sure that the opinion we are endeavoring to stifle is a false opinion...

All silencing of discussion is an assumption of infallibility....

Ages are no more infallible than individuals; every age having held many opinions which subsequent ages have deemed not only false but absurd; and it is as certain that many opinions now general will be rejected by future ages....

The only way in which a human being can make some approach to knowing the whole of a subject, is by hearing what can be said about it by persons of every variety of opinion, and studying all modes in which it can be looked at by every character of mind. No wise man ever acquired his wisdom in any mode but this....

The beliefs which we have most warrant for have no safeguard to rest on but a standing invitation to the whole world to prove them unfounded....

To call any proposition certain, while there is any one who would deny its certainty if permitted, but who is not permitted, is to assume that we ourselves and those who agree with us are the judges of certainty, and judges without hearing the other side....

Men are not more zealous for truth than they are for error, and a sufficient application of legal or even social penalties will generally succeed in stopping the propagation of either....

However unwilling a person who has a strong opinion may admit the possibility that his opinion may be false, he ought to be moved by the consideration that, however true it may be, if it is not fully, frequently, and fearlessly discussed, it will be a dead dogma, not a living truth.

I would like to point out to younger readers that John Stuart Mill lived in an era that was not sensitive to terms many people today consider sexist. The words *man* and *mankind* were often used in his work as synonyms for *people* and *humankind*.

A pitfall to avoid in considering alternative points of view is that of regarding your own point of view as being merely common sense and the most rational stance, and the point of view of others as being only opinion and naturally wrong. It may be that the opinion of others is correct and that yours is in error.

Another pitfall to avoid is that of closing your mind to the opinions of those whose views differ from yours. The best way to approach a dialogue is to make your primary purpose that of understanding the mind and arguments of the other person and not that of enlightening him or her with your solutions. One learns more by listening than by speaking.

It is my hope that after reading this book you will have a deeper understanding of the issues debated and will appreciate the complexity of even seemingly simple issues when good and honest people disagree. This awareness is particularly important in a democratic society such as ours, where people enter into public debate to determine the common good. People with whom you disagree should not be regarded as enemies, but rather as friends who suggest a different path to a common goal.

ANALYZING SOURCES OF INFORMATION

The Opposing Viewpoints Series uses diverse sources; magazines, journals, books, newspapers, statements and position papers from a wide range of individuals and organizations. These sources help in the development of a mindset that is open to the consideration of a variety of opinions.

The format of the Opposing Viewpoints Series should help you answer the following questions.

1. *Are you aware that three of the most popular weekly news magazines, Time, Newsweek, and U.S. News and World Report are not totally objective accounts of the news?*
2. **Do you know there is no such thing as a completely objective author, book, newspaper or magazine?**
3. **Do you think that because a magazine or newspaper article is unsigned it is always a statement of facts rather than opinions?**
4. **How can you determine the point of view of newspapers and magazines?**
5. **When you read do you question an author's frame of reference (political persuasion, training, and life experience)?**

Many people finish their formal education unable to cope with these basic questions. They have little chance to understand the social forces and issues surrounding them. Some fall easy victims to demagogues preaching solutions to problems by scapegoating minorities with conspiratorial and paranoid explanations of complex social issues.

I do not want to imply that anything is wrong with authors and publications that have a political slant or bias. All authors have a frame of reference. Readers should understand this. You should also understand that almost all writers have a point of view. An important skill in reading is to be able to locate and identify a point of view. This series gives you practice in both.

DEVELOPING BASIC THINKING SKILLS

A number of basic skills for critical thinking are practiced in the discussion activities that appear throughout the books in the series. Some of the skills are:

Locating a Point of View The ability to determine which side of an issue an author supports.

Evaluating Sources of Information The ability to choose from among alternative sources the most reliable and accurate source in relation to a given subject.

Distinguishing Between Primary and Secondary Sources The ability to understand the important distinction between sources which are primary (original or eyewitness accounts) and those which are secondary (historically removed from, and based on, primary sources).

Separating Fact from Opinion The ability to make the basic distinction between factual statements (those which can be demonstrated or verified empirically) and statements of opinion (those which are beliefs or attitudes that cannot be proved).

Distinguishing Between Prejudice and Reason The ability to differentiate between statements of prejudice (unfavorable, preconceived judgments based on feelings instead of reason) and statements of reason (conclusions that can be clearly and logically explained or justified).

Identifying Stereotypes The ability to identify oversimplified, exaggerated descriptions (favorable or unfavorable) about people and insulting statements about racial, religious or national groups, based upon misinformation or lack of information.

Recognizing Ethnocentrism The ability to recognize attitudes or opinions that express the view that one's own race, culture, or group is inherently superior, or those attitudes that judge another race, culture, or group in terms of one's own.

It is important to consider opposing viewpoints. It is equally important to be able to critically analyze those viewpoints. The discussion activities in this book will give you practice in mastering these thinking skills.

Using this book, and others in the series, will help you develop critical thinking skills. These skills should improve your ability to better understand what you read. You should be better able to separate fact from opinion, reason from rhetoric. You should become a better consumer of information in our media-centered culture.

A VALUES ORIENTATION

Throughout the Opposing Viewpoints Series you are presented conflicting values. A good example is *American Foreign Policy*. The first chapter debates whether foreign policy should be based on the same kind of moral principles that individuals use in guiding their personal actions, or instead be based primarily on doing what best advances national interests, regardless of moral implications.

The series does not advocate a particular set of values. Quite the contrary! The very nature of the series leaves it to you, the reader, to formulate the values orientation that you find most suitable. My purpose, as editor of the series, is to see that this is made possible by offering a wide range of viewpoints which are fairly presented.

David L. Bender
Opposing Viewpoints Series Editor

RELIGION AND HUMANITY

"Religion, after all, is the serious business of the human race."
Arnold Toynbee, *Civilization on Trial*.

Religion, the belief in a divine or supernatural power, is a universal cultural trait among humans. It cuts across time and space. From prehistory to the present, from the inner sanctums of primeval rain forests to the main thoroughfares of overpopulated cities, a staggering majority of human beings have been and still are prepared to accept belief in a supernatural force superior to themselves. The nature and names given these forces have varied greatly. The ways in which they are worshipped also have varied. But the unquestionable fact remains that most of humankind have always sought answers to unanswerable questions from powers beyond earthly knowledge. No less a thinker than Albert Einstein once acknowledged that his idea of God included "the presence of a superior reasoning power... revealed in the incomprehensible universe."

The universality of religion is understandably equaled by the influence it has had upon events and people. Many historians will agree that some of the bloodiest wars fought in history have been waged in the name of religion. On the other hand, many also will agree that many outstanding and fervent examples of individual or group charity and self-sacrifice can be traced to religious motives. Yet, whether outrage or humanitarianism, both are indications of the tremendous passions which religious belief can generate in people.

The prominent role religion has played in history and in individual lives has given rise to countless and relevant questions which social scientists, philosophers and theologians have been debating for centuries. What is the origin of humankind's religious "instinct?" How did the concept of God originate? Why does evil exist in a world created by a benevolent God? These and others are questions which can never be answered with certainty. In the final analysis, religious belief depends upon faith and faith, as St. Augustine wrote, "is to believe... what we do not see." Yet the debates continue, a fact which, perhaps more than all others, underlines the significance of religion in all of our lives.

It is because of the important role which religion has had in the lives of individuals and in the flow of history that this anthology has been assembled. The authors of the twenty-one viewpoints contained herein represent many different religious and secular persuasions. The questions debated range from seminal issues such as the origins of religion to the contemporary issue of the role of women in churches. The editors recognize that many of the issues may be considered controversial. However, the editors also believe that to shirk from relevant questions simply because they are too controversial is at best, foolish, and at worst, dishonest.

While reading this book, or any other which deals with the many sides of religion and human experience, the reader would do well to turn once again to the words of St. Augustine. If the existence or absence of a divine and supernatural force at work in the world could be proven beyond all doubt, this volume of opposing viewpoints would be unnecessary. However, that not being so, we are left with this observation: To believe or disbelieve both require an enormous leap of faith.

Chapter 1

Religion and human experience

What is the Origin of Religion?

> *"It was from the minds of ... primitive people that conceptions of Gods, Demons, Devils ... and all of the unseen manipulators of human destinies were imagined."*

Religion Originated in Primitive Minds

James Hervey Johnson

James Hervey Johnson (Born 1901) has devoted most of his adult life to furthering the cause of atheism. A veteran of WW II, Johnson has been president of the Atheist Association (the oldest organization of its kind in America) since 1963 and is president of the National League for the Separation of Church and State. In the following viewpoint, Johnson contends that religions were developed in ancient times when people "knew nothing of modern science... and mental horizons were restricted."

Consider the following questions while reading:

1. According to Johnson, when did the Jewish, Christian and Mohammedan religions ultimately originate?
2. Give some examples of the state of knowledge in the period of which Johnson is writing.
3. Johnson seems to be implying that if knowledge of science and the world had been greatly developed in earliest times, there might be no religions today. Do you agree? Why or why not?

James Hervey Johnson, *Superior Men.* Reprinted with permission of the author and through the courtesy of The Truth Seeker Co., Inc., Box 2832, San Diego, CA 92112.

Most religions with followings of any size were developed by primitive uneducated people hundreds of thousands of years ago. Nearly all new religions are based on those more primitive.

RELIGIONS' ROOTS

The Jewish religion has roots purportedly 6000 years old. The Christian religion is based on purported happenings some 1900 years ago and is an off-shoot of the basic Semitic or Jewish religion, which was probably a mixture of earlier smatterings of philosophy from the still more ancient Assyrians, Chaldeans, Egyptians, and Hindu religions and philosophies.

Our religious books and ideas have been carried down from those remote times and we are expected to follow the teachings and alleged orders of gods issued from 2000 to 10,000 years ago.

SOMETHING BORROWED, NOTHING NEW

There have been but few original systems of religion in the world; the later have borrowed from the earlier, and appropriated pre-existing dogmas, legends, rites, and superstitions. This has been the rule in all ages.

D. M. Bennett, *World's Sages, Thinkers and Reformers*

LIMITED KNOWLEDGE

Those ancient writers knew nothing of modern science. They had no telescopes to learn of astronomy. They did not realize that there are millions of stars. They had no scientific instruments. Their education was primitive. Only a few could read and write the tedious characters that stood for writings. Priests and preachers were almost the only scribes. The common people knew little except what they were told by their rulers.

Mental horizons were restricted by lack of communication with other peoples. Those who wrote the Bible didn't know that the earth was round or that America existed. They knew nothing of the north pole or the south pole. The flood of their own district was a flood of the whole world to them. Everyone they knew was in the flood, because only people they knew were nearby. Airplanes, trains, autos, and steamships were unknown. Roads were trails, and travel was by horse or camel back or by oxen, ass, or on foot. Twenty miles travel in a day was a long journey.

For such reasons few people ever got far from home. There was no mail system. The one we have today was founded about 1840. Rulers could send messengers running in relays but one auto today can cover more territory in a half hour that the runners did then in a whole day.

There were no magazines, daily papers, or public libraries. There was no radio. A man's own village, or the company of his fellow herdsman was almost his only opportunity for obtaining knowledge.

PARTIALLY CORRECT?

Godism was invented in the earliest days of man's ignorance. It is incredible that primitive man guessed wrongly about everything else, but discovered the truth about the origin of life.

American Atheist's Association

THE PRIMITIVE MIND

Man's mentality was poorly developed. There was little opportunity for mental development. Primitive minds had no store of scientific knowledge to draw from. They speculated and guessed at the facts of life. The more intelligent classes had more time for leisure and more time for imagining how the world began, what the controlling forces were, and what people should do. The average man's vocabulary was limited. Primitive races of today in the lands where our religions originated are among the most backward on earth.

It was from the minds of such untutored primitive people that conceptions of gods, demons, devils, genii, angels, and all of the unseen manipulators of human destinies were imagined. Are we then so undeveloped mentally that we must rely on the imaginings of ignorant, backward minds of primitive peoples, just emerging from savagery, to determine the cause of our lives and thoughts in these days of scientific development and opportunities for study and knowledge?

Intelligent persons do not accept their teachings.

"It was God who planted in the human heart the desire for personal flowering and growth."

Religion Is a Gift Of God

Alfred McBride

The Reverend Alfred McBride is the former Executive Director of the National Forum of Religious Education, a branch of the National Catholic Education Association. Currently, he lectures extensively before Catholic organizations and at colleges and universities throughout the U.S. In the following viewpoint, Rev. McBride analyzes the views of Marx and Freud that religion was meant to keep the masses frightened and subdued. He concludes that on the contrary, religion has made people "free".

Consider the following questions while reading:

1. How does the author respond to the criticism of religion by Marx and Freud?
2. According to McBride, what message has Jesus brought to people?

Alfred McBride, "Real Religious Belief Opens Door to Freedom," *The Catholic Bulletin,* March 25, 1977. Reprinted with permission of National Catholic News Service.

Karl Marx claimed that religious belief enslaved people. It was the opium of the people. It dulled their ambition and prevented them from being full human beings. In particular, the working classes would never try to fight for personal and economic freedom so long as they clung to religious belief which moved them to find pie in the sky since they were not finding much pie on earth.

CRITICISMS OF RELIGION

Freud taught a similar doctrine. In his mind, religious belief frightened people to the point where they were too scared to act. It filled people with so much fear that they were imprisoned by their anxieties and so they lost their freedom to act. As far as Freud was concerned religious belief, by inducing excessive guilt, was responsible for the multitude of neurotic obsessions he found in his patients.

THE IMPORTANCE OF BELIEF

Belief is a God-given gift. You don't acquire it, though you can predispose yourself to receive it. The whole merit of believing—as St. Augustine wrote—is that it's a gratuitous act beyond reason's reach. If reason could prove everything, we wouldn't have any merit at all in believing.

Mortimer Adler, *U.S. Catholic,* October, 1980

These criticisms of religious belief by Marx and Freud possess some validity. They were observing an approach to religious belief that was misguided, far from the kind advised by the Bible and divorced from the loving call asked for by Jesus. They witnessed a religious belief that was wedded to the false idea of an angry God who was presumably loathe to forgive, and a God who was apparently not interested in the earthly happiness and fulfillment of people in this world.

It is for these reasons, among many others, that it was thought by some that religious belief could not help people to move toward personal freedom and fulfillment. According to the wrong view of religious belief, God wanted to keep people like children— and naughty ones at that. Following this erroneous perception, it was thought that God had no interest in the maturing of human beings. He was supposed to exact fearsome obedience which allowed for no individual thinking and permitted no growth in personal judgment.

Blowing Beans at Gibraltar

Artist: Jack Hamm. Reprinted with permission of Religious Drawings, Inc.

Without a doubt this view of God and religious belief was used to keep people immature, to prevent them from breaking out of the limits of their class or from taking a wholesome, critical view of life. It was meant to herd them together as passive sheep and quell any ambitious desires that might rise in their hearts. Jesus had said that one must become again like a little child to enter the kingdom of heaven. The false view of religious belief misinterpreted this word of Christ to mean that people ought to be childish and not think for themselves.

RELIGIOUS BELIEF MEANS FREEDOM

Actually, real religious belief means freedom for the human person. Far from wanting us to forget earthly joy and fulfillment, God wants precisely that for us. When God made the first man and woman, he put them in the garden of happiness and fulfillment. Eden was no slave den. God asked Adam and Eve to trust Him and believe in Him so that their fulfillment and hopes would expand and grow. It was their sin—their inability to believe in Him—that brought about their loss of earthly happiness.

It was God who planted in the human heart the desire for personal flowering and growth. Why would genuine belief in Him bring about the opposite? It was God who said that we are made in His image. Is not His image one of beauty, hope, love and freedom? It is unbelief, expressed in sin, that produces the loss of earthly happiness here and hereafter. In the life of unbelief there is no pie in the sky–or pie on earth.

When Jesus came, He preached that belief in Him would bring one to enter the kingdom of God. He brought the Good News Gospel to the poor, the lonely, the oppressed. He announced an eternal life that could begin here on earth and be continued in the hereafter. He came to liberate the captives, console the lonely, give sight to the blind, hearing to the deaf and mobility to the crippled. Now this is freedom, not slavery. Belief in Him caused freedom in the believer.

Jesus treated people like adults and expected them to act that way. At no time did He try to compel, force or intimidate the persons to whom He preached and spoke. He, the Son of God, revered the image of God in all those whom he met. He wanted to give people the thrill of experiencing freedom. He gave them space in which to move and grow. He knew how to make people understand that God's main interest in them was in their personal good and happiness. God was always loving and forgiving and ready to help people overcome obstacles. Jesus promised freedom from sin and guilt and hopelessness. Real religious believers know this. They are truly "free" people in this world.

"The conception of divinity seems to me... to be a false one."

Religion Was Invented To Answer Unanswerable Questions

Julian S. Huxley

During his lifetime, Sir Julian S. Huxley (1887-1975) enjoyed the reputation of being one of the world's foremost biologists, humanists and philosophers. The grandson of Thomas H. Huxley (a famous 19th century scientist) and the brother of Aldous Huxley (a leading novelist and philosopher), Sir Julian wrote over forty books on scientific and philosophical topics and was in constant worldwide demand as a lecturer. In the following viewpoint, he articulates an opinion widely held among secular humanists, namely, that it was the backward state of knowledge in earlier times which gave rise to the belief in gods and religious concepts.

Consider the following questions while reading:

1. **How would you interpret Sir Julian's story about the philosopher, the theologian and the black cat?**
2. **How does the author answer the question, "Who or what rules the universe?"**
3. **Do you agree with the author's arguments? Why or why not?**

Abridged from "Life Can Be Worth Living" (pp. 288-293) (under the title "Man's Soaring Destiny") in *Man Stands Alone* by Julian S. Huxley. Reprinted by permission of Harper & Row, Publishers, Inc.

I do not believe that there is any absolute of truth, beauty, morality, or virtue, whether emanating from an external power or imposed by an internal standard. But this does not drive me to the curious conclusion, fashionable in certain quarters, that truth and beauty and goodness do not exist, or that there is no force or value in them.

I believe that there are a number of questions that it is no use our asking, because they can never be answered. Nothing but waste, worry or unhappiness is caused by trying to solve insoluble problems. Yet some people seem determined to try. I recall the story of the philosopher and the theologian. The two were engaged in disputation and the theologian used the old quip about a philosopher being like a blind man, in a dark room, looking for a black cat—which wasn't there. "That may be," said the philosopher, "but the theologian would have found it..."

THE NATURAL LAW OF RELIGION

You think religions are constant things? inflexible and solid and born full-grown? Religions evolve. They grow out of a need, just like any other natural phenomenon, and they follow the same natural laws. They are born, grow, have sons, and illegitimate sons, and die.

From Here To Eternity, James Jones

UNANSWERED QUESTIONS

I do not believe in the existence of a god or gods. The conception of divinity seems to me, though built up out of a number of real elements of experience, to be a false one, based on the quite unjustifiable postulate that there must be some more or less personal power in control of the world. We are confronted with forces beyond our control, with incomprehensible disasters, with death, and also with ecstasy, with a mystical sense of union with something greater than our ordinary selves, with sudden conversion to a new way of life, with the burden of guilt and sin. In theistic religions all these elements of actual experience have been woven into a unified body of belief and practice in relation to the fundamental postulate of the existence of a god or gods.

I believe this fundamental postulate to be nothing more than the result of asking a wrong question: "Who or what rules the universe?" So far as we can see, it rules itself, and indeed the whole analogy with a country and its ruler is false. Even if a god does exist behind or above the universe as we experience it, we can have no knowledge of such a power; the actual gods of historical religions are only the personifications of impersonal facts of nature and of facts of our inner mental life.

Similarly with immortality. With our present faculties we have no means of giving a categorical answer to the question whether we survive death, much less the question of what any such life after death will be like. That being so, it is a waste of time and energy to devote ourselves to the problem of achieving salvation in the life to come...

OTHER BELIEFS

But if God and immortality be repudiated, what is left? That is the question usually thrown at the atheist's head. The orthodox believer likes to think that nothing is left. That, however, is

Cover of September, 1980 issue of *The American Atheist* magazine, Vol. 22, No. 9.

because he has only been accustomed to think in terms of his orthodoxy.

In point of fact, a great deal is left.

That is immediately obvious from the fact that many men and women have led active, or self-sacrificing, or noble, or devoted lives without any belief in God or immortality, Buddhism in its uncorrupted form has no such belief; nor did the great nineteenth-century agnostics; nor do the orthodox Russian Communists; nor did the Stoics. Of course, the unbelievers have often been guilty of selfish or wicked actions; but so have the believers. And in any case that is not the fundamental point. The point is that without these beliefs men and women may yet possess the mainspring of full and purposive living, and just as strong a sense that existence can be worth while as is possible to the most devout believers.

SCIENCE PROVIDES ANSWERS

I would say that this is much more readily possible today than in any previous age. The reason lies in the advances of science.

No longer are we forced to accept the external catastrophes and miseries of existence as inevitable or mysterious; no longer are we obliged to live in a world without a history, where change is only meaningless. Our ancestors saw an epidemic as an act of divine punishment; to us it is a challenge to be overcome, since we know its causes and that it can be controlled or prevented. The understanding of infectious disease is entirely due to scientific advance. To take a very recent happening, so is our understanding of the chemical basis of nutrition, which holds out new possibilities of health and energy to the human race. So is our understanding of earthquakes and storms; if we cannot control them, we at least do not have to fear them as evidence of God's anger.

A VIVID IMAGINATION

All superstitions, whether labeled "religion" or belonging to the "broken-mirror" class, start as a mere imaginary explanation for something not understood, and that is all they are.

Man, Father Of The Gods, Kenneth C. Dick

Some, at least, of our internal miseries can be lightened in the same way. Through knowledge derived from psychology, children can be prevented from growing up with an abnormal sense of guilt and so making life a burden both to themselves and to those with whom they come in contact. We are beginning to understand the psychological roots of irrational fear and cruelty; someday we shall be able to make the world a brighter place by preventing their appearance.

"Faith has such might because next to love it is the force most inherent in one's own awareness."

Religion Is the Fruit of Faith

Helen Keller

Helen Keller (1880-1968) was honored in her lifetime as "the world's first lady of courage." No one would dispute that accolade. Deaf, blind and unable to speak since the age of two, she died a world famous celebrity. With her friend and teacher Anne Sullivan at her side, she walked with kings, befriended presidents, authored books and received honorary degrees from universities as separate as Harvard and Delhi, India. It was through her infirmity that she discovered her greatest asset, a boundless faith. In the following viewpoint, she explains how faith led her to a "religion of optimism."

Consider the following questions while reading:

1. What do you think the author means by the thought, "Religion is the fruit of faith?"
2. What are some of the things faith gave rise to in Miss Keller's life?
3. In your opinion, is it possible to have religion without faith? Explain your answer.

Excerpts from "In the Garden of the Lord" by Helen Keller from *Masterpieces of Religious Verse,* edited by Charles L. Wallis. Copyright 1948 by Harper & Brothers. Reprinted by permission of Doubleday & Company, Inc.

FAITH—THE MEASURE OF THINGS

In a true religion, faith in the ultimate meaningfulness of existence, grounded in a God who transcends the caprices and contingencies of the physical order and who is capable of overcoming the chaos created by human sin, is the final security of the human spirit.

Reinhold Niebuhr, *Christianity and Crisis*

A simple childlike faith in a Divine Friend solves all the problems that come to us by land or sea. Faith teaches us to use our talent to the fullest extent, however slight they may be. Faith is a responsibility for us as well as a privilege...

Religion is the fruit of faith, and to ask for religion without faith is to ask for the flower without the seed. Many world religions have spread inspiring hope upon the earth, but one faith has been their tree just as good will is the one root of all truly beneficent activities.

POWER OF FAITH

Faith has such might because next to love it is the force most inherent in one's own awareness. It directs to the light when darkness prevails; it supplies incentive to action and converts ideas into realities. It fires the imagination, and this is essential, for one must envision the higher life and behave as if it were a fact before it can unfold. But though faith belongs to the future, its energy irradiates the present, just as the green leaf pigment—the delicate link between the sun and life—permeates the vegetable world.

Faith, like philosophy, endows me with a unity I miss in the chaos of material experience devoid of sight and hearing. But like everyone else I have eyes in my soul. Through faith I create the world I gaze upon; I make my own day and night, tint the clouds with iridescent fires, and behold! a midnight is strewn with other stars. It is faith which lights us into sustaining realities beyond those perceived by the physical senses.

Faith transmutes circumstance, time, condition and mood into vitality. This is why Christ's teaching was momentously effective nineteen centuries ago and still is so today among those who truly respond to it. Then we wake to see with new eyes and hear with new ears the beauty and harmony of God's real world.

A DIFFERENT VISION

I am blind and have never seen a rainbow, but I have been told of its beauty. I know that its beauty is always broken and incomplete. Never does it stretch across the heavens in full perfection. So it is with all things as we know them here below. Life itself is as imperfect and broken for every one of us as the span of the rainbow. Not until we have taken the step from life into Eternity shall we understand the meaning of Browning's words: "On earth the broken arcs; in the heaven, a perfect round."

The most important question is not the sort of environment we have but the kind of thoughts we think every day, the kind of ideals we are following; in a word, the kind of men and women we really are . . . Join the great company of those who make the barren places of life fruitful with kindness.

The joy of surmounting obstacles which once seemed unremovable, and pushing the frontier of accomplishment further—what joy is there like unto it? Keep your face to the sunshine and you cannot see the shadow.

BY GOD'S GRACE

In the 1980s, we are finding that God is not an antique myth; rather, belief in God is the best way we know for relating to the mystery and the paradox that lie at the very heart of life. For when all is said and done, when we reach the outer limit of reason and knowledge, by God's grace, the gaps in our understanding are filled with faith, with hope and, at last, even with love.

Charles P. Henderson, Jr., *The Christian Century*, January 21, 1981

GOD GIVES, GOD TAKES

The reason, I am sure, why God permitted me to lose both sight and hearing seems clear now—that through me He might cleave a rock unbroken before and let quickening streams flow through other lives desolate as my own once was. I believe that life is given to us so we may glow in love, and I believe that God is in me as the sun is in the color and fragrance of a flower—the Light in my darkness, the Voice in my silence.

It would be wonderful to find myself free from even a small part of my physical limitations... to walk around town alone... to come and go without a word to anyone . . . to read the newspapers without waiting, and pick out a pretty handkerchief or a becoming hat in the shops.

Artist: Jack Hamm. Reprinted with permission of Religious Drawings, Inc.

I trust, and nothing that happens disturbs my trust. I recognize the beneficence of the Power which we all worship as supreme—Order, Fate, the Great Spirit, Nature, God. I recognize this power in the sun that makes all things grow and keeps life afoot. I make a friend of this indefinable force, and straightway feel glad, brave, and ready for any lot heaven may decree for me. This is my religion of optimism.

DEFINING RELIGION

This activity will give you an opportunity to examine your concept of religion. It also will give you a chance to see how your classmates define religion.

Instructions

STEP 1

Working individually, each student should rank the following definitions of religion, assigning the number (1) to the definition that best describes the nature of religion. Assign the number (2) to the second best definition, and so on, until all the definitions have been ranked.

STEP 2

The class should break into groups of four to six students.

STEP 3

Each student should compare her/his rankings with others in the group and present reasons for the ranking.

STEP 4

The group as a whole should rank the definitions in the manner described above. If possible, attempt to reach a group consensus.

DEFINITIONS OF RELIGION TO BE RANKED

_____ 1. Religion is a sense of the sacred.

_____ 2. Religion is morality tinged with emotion.

_____ 3. Religion is whatever makes one whole.

_____ 4. Religion is the belief in a spiritual creator.

_____ 5. Religion is superstitious attempt to give life meaning.

_____ 6. Religion is membership in a community of believers.

_____ 7. Religion is fellowship with the unseen.

_____ 8. Religion is one's concern for the Ultimate.

_____ 9. Religion is neurosis.

_____ 10. Religion is one's explanation for the existence of the universe and human life.

_____ 11. Religion is the feeling of utter dependence upon the infinite reality, God.

_____ 12. _____
(if you wish you may add and rank a definition you think should be included.)

"Our gods and goddesses, our devils and witches, are to a large extent the projections of our parental figures."

An Anthropologist Explains Religions' Origins

Ashley Montagu

Ashley Montagu is one of the twentieth century's most famous and respected anthropologists. Born in London, England (1905), he immigrated to the United States where he received his Ph.D. in 1937 from Columbia University. During his long and distinguished career, Mr. Montagu has written over three dozen books dealing with both the biological and cultural aspects of humanity. In the following viewpoint from his *Immortality, Religion, and Morals,* he explains how "the objective forms we tend to give our religions are greatly influenced by our experience as persons."

Consider the following questions while reading:
1. In the author's opinion, how do personal experiences influence people's concepts of God?
2. How do the people of Bali view their gods? In what way does this view of their gods relate to their society?
3. According to Montagu, what may be said to explain the wide appeal of Christianity?

The anthropologist surveying the great variety of patterns of human experience as he finds them at the present time has great difficulty in reconstructing the history of that experience. But one thing is clear in the study of the religious experience: The universe is presented to every people as something of a mystery, a universe of transcendental but powerful forces. And in every people of which we have any knowledge we find the individual and the group striving to relate themselves to these powerful forces. Such cravings are found to be universal, and to this elementary subjective experience we usually give the name "spiritual..."

The anthropologist, as he has come closer to the person in the field, to the individual member of society, has found that the person in society at once feels close to and very far from his fellow man, but there is always the strongest desire to be related to one's fellow man. Human beings have devised no more successful means of achieving this relatedness to one's fellow human beings than religion. When there is combined the emotional experience of the world in which one finds oneself as mystery, with the craving to solve some part of that mystery by identification with the powers that be, with the feeling of relatedness and loneliness, one has something of the matrix out of which the religions of all people grow.

PERSONAL EXPERIENCES INFLUENCE RELIGION

Studies at home and in the field have turned up strong evidence suggesting that the objective forms we tend to give our religions are greatly influenced by our experience as persons. This ought to sound like a truism. I hope it does. For example, the experience of children within the family, with their parents in particular, would seen to be closely related to the kind of gods different peoples create. For to many of us it seems that our gods and goddesses, our devils and witches, are to a large extent the projections of our parental figures...

THE GODS OF BALI

Bateson and Mead found that in Bali child-rearing practices were highly correlated with religious ideas and practices. Attitudes toward children are projected upon the gods. In Bali the gods are thought of as the children of the people, and they address the people as "mama" and "papa." The people spoil and indulge their gods just as in many ways they do their children. But the children also receive a good deal of frustration, particularly during the lengthy nursing period at the mother's breast. The father, on the whole, is the more embracing and permissive parent. It is not surprising, therefore, to find the mother represented in ceremonial theatrical performances as the witch and the father as the kindly dragon who is opposed to the witch.

INFANTILE FANTASY

Freud proposed that a paternalistic God is partly our projection as adults of our perceptions of our fathers when we were infants.

Broca's Brain, Carl Sagan

CHRISTIANITY

More recent studies in the field tend to support such correlations between parental discipline and the forms of religious belief. But we don't have to leave home in order to make this kind of analysis. The history and being of Christianity will serve our purposes very well. Christ was born into a society in which its dominant patriarchal structure gave the father tyrannical power over his family. This is well brought out in the Old Testament. The god of the Old Testament is a tyrannical father. In keeping with the subservient position of women among the Old Testament Jews, there are no female gods or minor female deities in the Jewish religion. The yearning for a loving father, which all children develop who have not had one, is to be seen expressed in the teaching and conduct of Christ. It may be suspected that the wide appeal which Christianity has had has in part been due to the fact that the central figure constitutes a father-image of love, a god of love. A god of love who, in keeping with the repressed fears of those who have been disciplined by tyrannical fathers, loves his children so much that he is even willing to sacrifice his only begotten son for them. Sons who have been sacrificed by their own fathers and who, as fathers themselves, may sacrifice their own sons, understandably find something attractive and satisfying in such a conception. For here one can at once have a father who is genuinely a father of love, a father whom one wished one's own father could have been, together with a filial relationship that is reminiscent of one's own and that may unconsciously be realized in relation to one's son...

In order to make the world intelligible to himself, man creates it anew in terms of his own experience; he brings the world, as it were, under domestication. The figures he projects into it are images compounded of the moral necessities that the authority figures of his experience, whether in the form of parents, teachers, or conscience, have urged upon him.

38

"It is obvious that our beliefs today must be consistent with our picture of the world."

The Four Sources of Religious Beliefs

Randolph Crump Miller

Horace Bushnell Professor of Christian Nurture at Yale University's Divinity School, Randolph Crump Miller is one of America's leading Christian educators. He has written nineteen books and has had numerous articles published in religious journals. As a contemporary religious writer, his ideas have influenced the religious thought of a generation of readers. In the following viewpoint, he carefully outlines the origins of Christian belief.

Consider the following questions while reading:

1. **List the four major sources from which, according to the author, Christian beliefs are derived.**
2. **Briefly explain each of the four sources.**
3. **What does the author mean by the following: "Beliefs held to be true in one century are reformulated, reinterpreted, enriched, or perhaps discarded in the next?**

Randolph Crump Miller, *This We Can Believe*. New York: Hawthorn Books, Inc., 1976. Reprinted with permission of the author.

There are four major sources of our beliefs as Christians. They come to us from tradition, from the Bible, from nonreligious knowledge, and from our common human experiences.

TRADITION

The first and primary source of belief is tradition. Christianity is an historical religion, and no one who partakes of the heritage of Western civilization can miss fully this influence. The average Christian today grows up in a particular cultus, and in gaining a sense of the ethos of one's own religious body one inherits beliefs, attitudes, and ideals which determine one's general religious outlook. Those outside Christianity do not remain free from its influence. To a certain extent this is a good thing, for it is patently impossible for all people to start over again in each generation without the benefit of this heritage...

The champion of tradition has been the church, and throughout the ages it has been the church which has preserved Christian doctrine from destruction. We could wish that the church might have saved more of the early Christian writings than those found in the New Testament, but the church is to be thanked for what was saved. The church has been interested in conserving the past rather than in creating the future, so that it has not always served the real needs of humanity. We need to steer a central course between the bonds of tradition and the snares of our individual conceits, and the church today needs to be both more careful and more courageous in its handling of the past.

Tradition is an invaluable storehouse of expressions of religious beliefs and practices, but in itself it contains only suggestions of possible beliefs as guides to action. It contributes to modern beliefs and faith only as it is rephrased into the vocabulary of modern communication and is verified and validated in the present. To some people such changes in both language and concepts may seem revolutionary, whether in the field of liturgy or social action. At the same time, simply because it is tradition, we deserve to give it considerate treatment and to gain perspective on the present through the past. We must not be too impatient with these older concepts and practices just because they do not seem to fit the immediate situation.

THE BIBLE

A second source of belief and particular source of tradition which is binding to some extent on all Christians is the Bible. The record of the experiences and beliefs found there provides a basis in history for almost all traditional beliefs. But even in this sacred realm, the beliefs must be retested, restated, and dressed in modern concepts and translations. The reason the Bible is

BIBLE AS AUTHORITY

The reason the Bible is normative for Christian beliefs is not because it has supernatural authority, but because the experiences and testings of people through the ages have validated certain portions as God's revelation.

Randolph Crump Miller
Copyright, Richard C. Miller. Reprinted with permission.

normative for Christian beliefs is not because it has supernatural authority, but because the experiences and testings of people through the ages have validated certain portions as God's revelation. Thus, it comes to have a unique authority as we understand more fully its origin and purpose, but even biblical beliefs cannot become a basis for faith without independent verification in present experience.

Within the Bible, the teachings of the New Testament have usually been treated with less critical acumen than those of the Old Testament, but even the Old Testament studies by Christian scholars have not often done justice to the Jewishness of Old Testament religion. The protrayal of Jesus as the Christ in traditional doctrines has not always done justice to the New Testament evidence. For example, it cannot be shown that all of Jesus' reported teachings are free from error, and if he was wrong, for example, in his specific statements concerning the end of the world, it is conceivable that he was wrong on other counts. We revere him and his teachings, and we find in him the center of our devotion but we have no right to accept beliefs about him uncritically. Jesus' teachings have been ratified by experience many times, and even where many have doubted him subsequent events have shown him to be right after all, but it is difficult to avoid the conclusion that he may have been wrong occasionally. So we must apply the same critical discernment to

Reprinted from *Catholic Twin Circle*.

the discovery and validating of his teachings and the teachings about him as we do to all biblical and church traditions.

SECULAR KNOWLEDGE

Third, general secular knowledge provides data which may have religious significance. It was not an accident that Thomas Aquinas built his theology on the secular philosophy of Artistotle, or that process theologians today build on the philosophy of Alfred North Whitehead. We must know the world if we are to have any accurate knowledge of God. We do not identify God with the world, as in pantheism, but as we know the world we also come to know God. When we spell out our way of looking on the world, we are setting up the environment for our religious thinking. In other words, religion without metaphysics is impossible except as a theological abstraction. If we cannot find God in the order of the skies or the breaking of an atom, we are not likely to find God at prayer meeting or at mass. As our inherited beliefs were fitted into what is now an outmoded metaphysical framework, so it is obvious that our beliefs today must be consistent with our picture of the world.

COMMON RELIGIOUS EXPERIENCE

The fourth source of our beliefs is our interpretation of common human experience, particularly as it is exemplified in personal experience. As in the fields of music or painting, the meaning and validity of religion lie in personal appreciation and verification. By their fruits you shall know them and by your fruits shall you know yourself. Religion must be grounded in the experience of persons. Of course, we must have objective tests by which to measure our experiences and norms by which to judge them. Our criteria emerge from joint efforts to evaluate experience.

We may take the authority of the expert in science, but in the field of religion even the authority of the expert cannot make belief live. The final experiment is that of life itself, and no one can do this by proxy. Each individual must make it for one's self or take the consequences. It can be postponed, but not indefinitely. Sometimes the beginning of the experience comes in the normal process of growth, but frequently it takes a crisis which demands a decision, and this opens the door to the experiment which must be made.

Beliefs held to be true in one century are reformulated, reinterpreted, enriched, or perhaps discarded in the next. In no field of human knowledge, not even religion, are there fixed truths. Static beliefs cannot apply for very long to a process which is constantly changing, cannot take account of new experiences or even of new perspectives on familiar data, and cannot point to future discoveries.

DISTINGUISHING BETWEEN FACT AND OPINION

This discussion activity is designed to help develop the *critical thinking skill of distinguishing between fact and opinion.* Consider the following quotation as an example. "Christianity is one of the major world religions and has had a profound influence upon the course of world history." The preceding statement is a fact which no historian or theologian, of any religious persuasion, would deny. But let us consider a statement which attempts to judge the influence of Christianity upon civilization. "The world would be a better place were it not for Christianity." Such a statement is clearly an expressed opinion. The good or bad effects Christianity has had, is having or will have upon humanity obviously depend upon one's point of view. An atheist will view Christianity from a far different perspective than will a devout Christian.

PART I

Instructions

Some of the following statements are taken from this book and some have other origins. Consider each statement carefully. Mark *O* for any statement you feel is an opinion or interpretation of facts. Mark *F* for any statement you believe is a fact. Then discuss and compare your judgments with those of other class members.

O = Opinion
F = Fact

_____ 1. Freud proposed that a fatherly God is partly our projection as adults of our perceptions of our fathers when we were infants.

_____ 2. It was God who planted in the human heart the desire for personal flowering and growth.

_____ 3. It was fear of the unknown which led prehistoric peoples to develop belief in God and form religions.

_____ 4. The religious indoctrination we receive in childhood shapes the course of our future religious thinking and beliefs.

_____ 5. Animal wisdom proves that there exists a good Creator who infused instinct into otherwise helpless little creatures.

_____ 6. Until someone can _prove_ the existence of God, belief in God is purely an act of faith.

_____ 7. Women should have the same religious opportunities as men.

_____ 8. An attractive female minister conducting a religious service would be a distraction to the males in the congregation.

_____ 9. Christianity and Judaism are sexist religions.

_____ 10. It is possible for human beings to lead meaningful lives and to serve their fellow humans without having religious commandments.

_____ 11. In the final analysis, religion is an instrument in a person's search for his or her identity.

_____ 12. _All_ religions are different paths to the same Truth.

_____ 13. The church improves society.

PART II

Instructions

STEP 1

The class should break into groups of four to six students.

STEP 2

Each small group should try to locate two statements of fact and two statements of opinion in this book.

STEP 3

Each group should choose a student to record its statements.

STEP 4

The class should discuss and compare the small groups' statements.

PART III

Instructions

STEP 1

Write a brief essay of at least two paragraphs on any aspect of "Religion and Human Experience." In your essay, be certain to include statements of both fact and opinion.

STEP 2

Each student should then exchange essays with one other member of the class. As you read your classmate's essay, underline and label statements you believe are fact and those you believe are opinion.

STEP 3

Return the essay you have underlined and labeled to the classmate who wrote it. See if that classmate agrees with your evaluation. If any disagreement exists, both students should attempt to justify their positions to each other.

BIBLIOGRAPHY OF USEFUL BOOKS

Peter Angeles, ed.	**Critiques of God.** New York: Prometheus Books. 1976.
Robert O. Ballou	**The Nature of Religion.** New York: Basic Books, 1968.
Paul Blanshard, ed.	**Classics of Free Thought.** New York: Prometheus Books.
Hiram Elfenbein	**Organized Religion.** New York: Philosophical Library, 1968.
Joseph Gaer	**How the Great Religions Began.** New York: The New American Library, 1956.
Roland Gammon, ed.	**All Believers Are Brothers.** Garden City, N.Y.: Doubleday and Company, 1969.
William J. Goode	**Religion among the Primitives.** New York: The Macmillan Company, 1969.
Andrew M. Greeley	**Unsecular Man: The Persistence of Religion.** New York: Schocken Books, 1972.
Bernard Haring	**Faith and Morality in the Secular Age.** Garden City, N.J.: Doubleday and Company, 1973.
William James	**The Varieties of Religious Experiences.** New York: The New American Library, 1958.
Eugene C. Kennedy	**Believing.** Garden City, N.Y.: Doubleday and Company, 1974.
Gerhard Lenski	**The Religious Factor.** Garden City, N.Y.: Doubleday and Company, 1961.
Elizabeth K. Nottingham	**Religion: A Sociological View.** New York: Random House, 1971.
Clark H. Pinnock	**Reason Enough: A Case for the Christian Faith.** Downers Grove, Illinois: InterVarsity Press, 1980.
Hans-Joachim Schoeps	**The Religions of Mankind.** Garden City, N.Y.: Doubleday and Company, 1966.
Harold H. Watts	**The Modern Reader's Guide to Religions.** New York: Barnes and Noble, 1964.
Donald A. Wells	**God, Man, and the Thinker: Philosophies of Religion.** New York: Random House, 1962.

Chapter **2**

Religion and human experience

Does God Exist?

"The belief in 'God' is reactionary and harmful."

God Is An Impossibility

Fred Woodworth

The *American Atheist* is a monthly magazine published in Austin, Texas. Dr. Madalyn Murray O'Hair, who spearheaded the court battle to have prayer prohibited in public schools, is the magazine's Editor-in-Chief. The *American Atheist* is essentially a journal of atheist news and thought. The following viewpoint, by Fred Woodworth, appeared in the September, 1977 issue of the magazine. It deals with atheism's central tenet, namely, that "there is no God."

Consider the following questions while reading:
1. **What is the author's attitude toward Christ?**
2. **List several of the author's arguments against the existence of God.**
3. **Do you note any flaws in Woodworth's arguments or logic? If so, what are they?**

Fred Woodworth, "There Is No God," *The American Atheist*, September 1977. Reprinted with permission of the publisher.

ETERNAL PUNISHMENT

Incredible it is to accept a God whose eternal torment (of sinners) makes the Nazis' lime-filled cars and gas chambers pale into nothingness in comparison.

A.G.N. Flew, "Does God Really Exist?," *Liberty,* January/February, 1977

There is no God. What is called "God", namely, a supposed-to-be all-knowing, everywhere present supreme wise spirit, CANNOT exist, for a number of reasons. I hope to be able to show to any reasonably open-minded person who will take the trouble to read my arguments (and who will not assume that I am an evil agent of "godless Communism"), that there is not the least reason to put any stock in the claims of persons who think such a supreme spirit exists.

TRADITION BOUND

Let me begin by noting that most of those who today think it is proper to believe in a god do so automatically, because others before them have done the same. That this is not a good reason for doing anything ought to be apparent to all. If, then, you happen to think already that my own claim in the title of this essay is wrong, won't you search your mind and think of when, if ever, anything BUT the automatic assumption of a god's existence was ever presented to you as a viable belief? Actually, the belief in a god has been traditional for many centuries, just as many other notions have been...

According to Christianity, two gods exist: the good god and the god of evil, the Devil. Thus, anybody could really choose which of the two to worship; but what if it could be shown that there was not, logically, any difference? Consider that the "good" god MUST be either totally powerless and superfluous, or else non-existent, since this god is necessarily either responsible for conditions being as they are today, or else powerless to prevent this. An ancient series of questions and answers inquires and concludes:

> **"Is god willing to prevent evil, but not able? Then he is not omnipotent.**
> **Is he able, but not willing? Then he is malevolent.**
> **Is he both able and willing? Then whence cometh evil?**
> **Is he neither able nor willing? Then why call him god?"**

Why believe in an ineffective or powerless god? Why believe in an evil god? One would be better off to worship the sun; at least the sun exists.

But Christianity, whose notion of a god prevails in our culture, makes other claims that he is wise, that he created the real world, that he is merciful, that he is a god responsible for beauty, that he knows everything.

And yet these qualities are not possible, either in combination with each other or separately. Can god think of a task he cannot accomplish? If so, then he has imagined a case in which he is not omnipotent. But if he cannot think of such a case, then he is not all-knowing.

If he was necessary to create the real world, in its infinite complexity, then who was necessary to create god, who is presumably still more complex?

BEAUTY AND UGLINESS

If he is responsible for beauty, he is likewise responsible for ugliness. Is there any justice in praising him for the beautiful, but keeping silent about the hideous? Some religionists seem to delight in ascribing to "God" the credit for having made apple trees in fields of green, under a blue sky; but where is their creator when we contemplate the fact of tapeworms?...

If he is wise, why did he not compose a coherent account of what he wanted mankind to do? The very god who, according to those believing in him, made every last electron spin in its orbit everywhere throughout the universe, still cannot write a clear, unmistakable volume of instruction to human beings who are supposed to follow his wishes. Instead, he gives us the Bible, a ridiculous jumble of ancient superstitions, contradictions, and vague, wandering narratives that show nothing so much as how senile the priests were who wrote them.

WHY CHRIST?

God according to the Bible, created the Devil. God, being all-knowing, must have known what the Devil would do; why, then, did he create him? Likewise, if god really wanted to "save" mankind, why not do it by the simple methods already used when creating the world — namely, by just snapping his fingers? God seems to be given to utilizing methods of senseless complexity: he wants a world of goodness, yet creates the Devil; wants to help mankind, but only sends among us an agent who spreads confusion and helps nothing, absolutely nothing. Christ's so-called purpose — to save man

51

— is futile, since a god who could create the cosmos could surely "save man" without resorting to a ridiculous ritual in Palestine. Further, from the evidence of the Holy Wars and Inquisitions carried out by those believing in Christianity, it must be concluded that Christ's advent was a major tragedy to the human species, since it has worsened considerably the lot of millions.

If the Bible was God's attempt to prove to mankind that he existed, then he must have wished for mankind to believe this. But, as the best way to make mankind believe in god would be for this god to publicly, unmistakably, make himself known to us, it is apparent that god's methods were lacking in intelligence. Thus, I myself can think of methods superior to those of

Cover of April, 1977 issue of *The American Atheist* magazine, Vol. 19, No. 4.

"God"; but a god so incompetent that any mere mortal can surpass his mind is an absurdity. God must not exist.

If god is just, why has he created a world of injustice? The reply that our world is a test by god to see which among us will do this or that, is a reply that is very poorly considered. Millions of young children are maimed or killed, or born with gruesome deformities — thus, god does not even have the sense to apply his test to all under equal conditions. Even the Driver's License Bureau is wiser than "God"!...

ETHNOCENTRIC BIAS

Now, some charge that our view of "God" is ethnocentric. They are anxious to bring in gods which do not create, control, or know anything, and which are completely powerless, futile intangibilities having no qualities of matter, energy, or even location. They wish to prove that "God" is a "process", or a "consciousness", or some other non-descript vagueness which neatly escapes having any properties assigned to itself so that detractors could discuss the logical implications of them. Conceptually speaking, it is meaningless to say that "God" is a process or a consciousness. But once this piece of verbal sleight-of-hand is let pass unchallenged, the modern religionist can point with triumph to things that do exist, such as processes, consciousnesses, and "prove" his "god" exists.

BRAINWASHING

How did each of us come by the religious convictions he now holds? Where and how did the idea of God come? Which came first, the belief in God or the hope of immortality? I am quite sure that you will agree with me that most of our religious ideas come to us through the happenstance of birth and environment. The religious indoctrination we receive in childhood pretty much shapes the course of our future religious thinking and beliefs.

Arthur Cromwell, *Why I Do Not Believe*

It works this way: First a religionist refuses to concede that he believes in the "old" god. His new god serves no purpose that he will define, so it cannot be attacked, but only denied. Evidently, then, religion has learned something from the attacks by us Atheists: it has learned to be non-specific. Thus, "God" is now "the wind", or something else. But we must point out that this is only an attempt to preserve the notion of a god after the substance has been destroyed. Lacking any separate function, such as being creator of the universe, etc., the idea of a god is completely to no purpose...

THERE IS NO GOD

We Atheists make a revolutionary claim: Nothing exists unless it can be proved to do so — the burden of proof being upon those who assert. The advance of the human intellect has been one long battle for this rational principle, against a vicious host of advocates of all kinds of nonexistent things: angels, humours, stellar spheres, dragons, ends of the earth where the explorer would drop off, warlocks and monsters, and so on — and, lastly, "God". He who is too weak to deny "God" perforce lives in a fantasy of unseen presences — the very walls may seethe with extraordinary witchery, and the neighbors turn into toads at midnight.

There is no god. As expressed by religions, the history of "God" is silly, unfactual, and contradictory. As set forth by theologians, the idea of "God" is an argument that assumes its own conclusions, and proves nothing. And as expressed socially, the belief in "God" is reactionary and harmful, standing forever in the way of betterment of the human condition. There is no god; there are only people who believe because others told them it was so. There is no god; there is only the real world with its ugliness and beauty and violence and peace and happiness and peaceful and happy, "God" won't do it. We will.

"The heavens declare the glory of God and the firmament showeth his handiwork."

God is the Only Possibility

A. Cressy Morrison

The belief held by some that a true scientist will have difficulty accepting a creator God is obviously based more on opinion than on firm evidence. A. Cressy Morrison (1884-1951) was a noted astronomer and president of the New York Academy of Sciences (1938-1939). A prolific writer on scientific topics, Dr. Morrison also used his narrative skills to show how nature supports the concept of God. The following viewpoint, an excerpt from his book, *Man Does Not Stand Alone*, illustrates this idea.

Consider the following questions while reading:

1. **List Morrison's seven reasons for his faith in God.**
2. **What examples does Morrison offer to illustrate how "animal wisdom speaks irresistibly of a good Creator?"**
3. **Which of Morrison's seven arguments do you feel is weakest? Which is strongest? Explain your answers.**

We are still in the dawn of the scientific age and every increase of light reveals more brightly the handiwork of an intelligent Creator...with a spirit of scientific humility and of faith grounded in knowledge we are approaching even nearer to an awareness of God.

For myself, I count seven reasons for my faith:

First... *By unwavering mathematical law we can prove that our universe was designed and executed by a great engineering Intelligence.*

Suppose you put ten pennies, marked from one to ten, into your pocket and give them a good shuffle. Now try to take them out in sequence from one to ten, putting back the coin each time and shaking them all again. Mathematically we know that your chance of first drawing number one is one to ten; of drawing one and two in succession, one to 100; of drawing one, two and three in succession, one in a thousand, and so on; your chance of drawing them all, from number one to number ten in succession, would reach the unbelievable figure of one chance in ten billion.

By the same reasoning, so many exacting conditions are necessary for life on the earth that they could not possibly exist in proper relationship by chance. The earth rotates on its axis one thousand miles an hour; if it turned at one hundred miles an hour, our days and nights would be ten times as long as now, and the hot sun would then burn up our vegetation each long day while in the long night any surviving sprout would freeze.

Again, the sun, source of our life, has a surface temperature

---

THE SOURCE OF ALL THINGS

When we understand that God is real, we begin to see the divine qualities everywhere. We can never doubt again. We trace all good back to its source, God — the song of a bird, the fidelity of a friend, the magnificent sounds of a symphony orchestra, the lines of a fine piece of architecture. All these hint the reality of God, for they express Him, and turn our thought to the supreme Being in which originate all law, order, and loveliness.

The Christian Science Monitor, September 8, 1973

of 12,000 degrees Fahrenheit, and our earth is just far enough away so that this "eternal fire" warms us *just enough and not too much!* If the sun gave off only one half its present radiation, we would freeze and if it gave half as much more, we would roast.

The slant of the earth, tilted at an angle of 23 degrees, gives us our seasons; if it had not been so tilted, vapors from the ocean would move north and south, piling up for us continents of ice. If our moon was, say, only 50 thousand miles away instead of its actual distance, our tides would be so enormous that twice a day all continents would be submerged; even the mountains would soon be eroded away...

Because of these and a host of other examples, there is not one chance in millions that life on our planet is an accident.

Second... *The resourcefulness of life to accomplish its purpose is a manifestation of all-pervading Intelligence.*

What life itself is, no man has fathomed. It has neither weight nor dimensions, but it does have force; a growing root will crack a rock. Life has conquered water, land and air, mastering the elements, compelling them to dissolve and reform their combinations.

Life, the sculptor, shapes all living things; an artist, it designs every leaf of every tree, and colors every flower. Life is a musician and has taught each bird to sing its love songs, the insects to call each other in the music of their multitudinous sounds. Life is a sublime chemist, giving taste to fruits and spices, and perfume to the rose, changing water and carbonic acid into sugar and wood, and, in so doing, releasing oxygen that animals may have the breath of life...

Who, then, has put it here?

Third... *Animal wisdom speaks irresistibly of a good Creator who infused instinct into otherwise helpless little creatures.*

The young salmon spends years at sea, then comes back to his own river, and travels up the very side of the river into which flows the tributary where he was born. What brings him back so precisely? If you transfer him to another tributary he will know at once that he is off his course and he will fight his way down and back to the main stream and then turn up against the current to finish his destiny accurately.

Even more difficult to solve is the mystery of eels. These amazing creatures migrate at maturity from all ponds and rivers everywhere — those from Europe across thousands of miles of ocean — all bound for the same abysmal deeps near Bermuda. There they breed and die. The little ones, with no apparent means of knowing anything except that they are in a wilderness of water, nevertheless start back and find their way not only to the very shore from which their parents came but thence to the rivers, lakes or little ponds — so that each body of water is always populated with eels. No American eel has ever been caught in Europe, no European eel in American waters. Nature has even delayed the maturity of the European eel by a year or more to make up for its longer journey. Where does the directing impulse originate?...

Fourth...*Man has something more than animal instinct—the power of reason.*

No other animal has ever left a record of its ability to count to ten, or even to understand the meaning of ten. Where instinct is like a single note of a flute, beautiful but limited, the human brain contains all the notes of all the instruments in the orchestra. No need to belabor this fourth point; thanks to human reason we can contemplate the possibility that we are what we are only because we have received a spark of Universal Intelligence.

Fifth... *Provision for all living is revealed in phenomena which we know today but which Darwin did not know—such as the wonders of genes.*

So unspeakably tiny are these genes that, if all of them responsible for all living people in the world could be put in one place, there would be less than a thimbleful. Yet these ultramicroscopic genes and their companions, the chromosomes, inhabit every living cell and are the absolute keys to all human, animal and vegetable characteristics. A thimble is a small place in which to put all the individual characteristics of two billions of human beings. However, the facts are beyond question. Well, then — how do genes lock up all the normal heredity of a multitude of ancestors and preserve the psychology of each in such an infinitely small space?

Here evolution really begins — at the cell, the entity which holds and carries the genes. How a few million atoms, locked up as an ultramicroscopic gene, can absolutely rule all life on earth is an example of profound cunning and provision that could emanate only from a Creative Intelligence; no other hypothesis will serve.

Sixth... *By the economy of nature, we are forced to realize that only infinite wisdom could have foreseen and prepared with such astute husbandry.*

Many years ago a species of cactus was planted in Australia as a protective fence. Having no insect enemies in Australia the cactus soon began a prodigious growth; the alarming abundance persisted until the plants covered an area as long and wide as England, crowding inhabitants out of the towns and villages, and destroying their farms. Seeking a defense, the entomologists scoured the world; finally they turned up an insect which lived exclusively on cactus, and would eat nothing else. It would breed freely, too; and it had no enemies in Australia. So animal soon conquered vegetable and today the cactus pest has retreated, and with it all but a small protective residue of the insects, enough to hold the cactus in check forever.

GOD'S CREATION

We start with what we can sense— the physical universe—and we find blunt proof that only a Supreme Creator could have fashioned it all together into such a wondrously unified whole. From the forces which bind atomic nuclei to the principles which run giant galaxies; from the fullness of earth to the emptiness of space; from the existence of law to the law of existence; from the beauty of creation to a mind which can comprehend it— all testify to the power of our God, all blazon forth the conclusive evidence of His existence.

"Why Does God Hide Himself," *The Plain Truth,* David Jon Hill

---

Such checks and balances have been universally provided. Why have not fast-breeding insects dominated the earth? Because they have no lungs such as man possesses; they breathe through tubes. But when insects grow large, their tubes do not grow in ratio to the increasing size of the body. Hence there never has been an insect of great size; this limitation on growth has held them all in check. If this physical check had not been provided, man could not exist. Imagine meeting a hornet as big as a lion!

Seventh... *The fact that man can conceive the idea of God is in itself a unique proof.*

The conception of God rises from a divine faculty of man,

59

unshared with the rest of our world — the faculty we call imagination. By its power, man and man alone can find the evidence of things unseen. The vista that power opens up is unbounded; indeed, as man's perfected imagination becomes a spiritual reality, he may discern in all the evidences of design and purpose the great truth that heaven is wherever and whatever; that God is everywhere and in everything but nowhere so close as in our hearts.

It is scientifically as well as imaginatively true, as the Psalmist said: *The heavens declare the glory of God and the firmament showeth His handiwork.*

"There simply is no proof for the existence of God."

Why I Don't Believe In God

Paul H. Beattie

Paul H. Beattie is the minister of All Souls Unitarian Church in Indianapolis and president of the Fellowship of Religious Humanists. He received his BD (Bachelor of Divinity) from the University of Chicago. Mr. Beattie has written widely on humanistic subjects, several of his articles having appeared in the journal *Religious Humanism*. He is currently completing work on his PhD in literature at the University of Chicago.

Consider the following questions while reading:

1. **List the three traditional proofs for the existence of God and briefly explain them.**
2. **According to Beattie, why does the ontological argument fail to prove that God exists?**
3. **In addition to the "three traditional proofs," what additional arguments are given which attempt to prove God's existence?**

This article first appeared in *The Humanist* January/February 1974 and is reprinted by permission.

The humanist is likely to be either an atheist or an agnostic. I am an agnostic leaning toward atheism. The agnostic says that he does not know if there is a God. I am an agnostic because no one at the present time can prove or disprove whether or not there is a cosmic spirit or mind at work in the universe. The atheist says either that he does not believe in God or that God does not exist. When he asserts that God does not exist, the atheist is making the same mistake as the theist — he is asserting something that cannot be proved...

THREE PROOFS

There are three traditional proofs or arguments for God's existence: the cosmological argument, the teleological argument, and the ontological argument. Since the time of Immanuel Kant in the eighteenth century, all of these proofs have been considered to be discredited.

The cosmological argument for God's existence holds that there must have been an original first cause of the universe. This assumes that the universe had a cause, or had a beginning, which is something we cannot know. To say that God has created the universe is to say nothing. It tells us nothing new about the universe or about God. It leads to an infinite regress because the next question would be, "What created God?" or "How did He begin?" If the answer is given that God has existed forever, one might just as well say that the universe has existed forever.

The teleological argument, which proves God's existence through purpose or design, is no more sure. Man increasingly has realized that the evidence of design that he sees is more a product of his mind than of the universe. The kind of balance and cooperation found in nature does not imply a divine intelligence. The structure of matter is enough to account for all that has happened on this planet. Matter is energy, and energy is matter. So far as we know everything that exists is a form of matter or energy. Given a hot cooling mass circling the sun, all else follows: the emergence of life out of inorganic material; the proliferation of life to fill every ecological niche; and the possibility that life could become symbolically self-conscious and therefore develop a new capacity for cultural transcendence and self-direction. That matter has an atomic structure and is alive with motion is no proof of a divine intelligence.

The ontological argument for God's existence is that, since the idea of God exists in the mind of man, there must be a God. How could the idea of God ever have arisen if it was not a reflection of some existing being or reality? Or, since we are able to imagine perfection, it must exist. These statements are, of course, absurd. Words are symbols that the mind can create and use at will. Thus words can symbolize things that do not exist. I can conceive of a pink elephant, but that does not mean that one exists in the real world.

Not only does the ontological argument fail, but attempts to reflect on the origin of the concept of God can often lead to atheism or agnosticism. The ancient Greek, Xenophanes of Colophon, writing around 530 B.C., said, "...if oxen (and horses) and lions had hands or could draw...and create works of art like those made by men, horses would draw pictures of gods like horses, and oxen of gods like oxen..." He also noted, "Ethiopians have gods with snub noses and black hair, Thracians have gods with grey eyes and red hair." Sigmund Freud's researches in the nineteenth century made it very evident that God is often the result of human needs or desires projected on the universe. For Freud, God was in effect an infantile dependence on an immature father projection! Freud's theory adequately accounts for the psychological potency of the God concept in human history. Anthropological studies have shown us how cultures have created and modified their gods according to their social needs.

IMPROBABLE POSSIBILITY

I do not pretend to be able to prove that there is no God. I equally cannot prove that Satan is a fiction. The Christian God may exist; so may the Gods of Olympus, or of ancient Egypt, or of Babylon. But no one of these hypotheses is more probable than any other: they lie outside the region of even probable knowledge, and therefore there is no reason to consider any of them.

Bertrand Russell, *What I Believe*

OTHER PROOFS

Several arguments for God's existence, beyond the three traditional proofs, have been advanced, but these also are destroyed by the acids of reason. Kant introduced the moral argument for God that now takes several forms. The fact that man is moral means that there must be a God, or else how could morality have arisen? Or, moral behavior ought to be rewarded by happiness, but this does not always happen, so there must be a God who ultimately rewards us beyond the grave. And, finally, human values seem to be built into the nature of things, so there must be a God. Such statements represent inadequate analysis and poor logic. Morality in man does not prove God's existence; it proves only that some men have a moral sensibility. We do not know that ultimately the good shall triumph in this life, and the possibility of a future existence is extremely doubtful. Wishing that a God would guarantee the moral order does not make God a reality...

AN ACT OF WILL

There simply is no proof for the existence of God. Any belief in God, then, held by a rational mind, must be on the basis of a leap of faith (or an act of will). But it is important for the humanist to note that *God's existence cannot be disproved.* One cannot disprove the existence of God. One cannot prove a universal negative. In any case, most of the new definitions of God are specifically formulated so as to be incapable of proof or disproof! Since the burden of proof for anything should rest with the affirmative, it is the responsibility of the believer in God to convince those who are skeptical. And, yet, it seems to me better not to assert that, because believers have failed to prove their point, God does not exist. We should remain humble before the unknown and unprovable. I like the stance of Sidney Hook, who says that he is still looking for God but has never found Him.

"No one would think a wrist watch could come into being without an intelligent designer. How much more incredible is it to believe that the universe...could have happened by chance?"

Why I Do Believe In God

Paul E. Little

From 1950 until his death in 1975, Paul E. Little served as staff evangelist with the Intervarsity Christian Fellowship. An Associate Professor of Evangelism at Trinity Evangelical Divinity School, Mr. Little was deeply committed to spreading Christian ideals and principles. He was a successful author whose works included *How to Give Away Your Faith* and the popular *Affirming the Will of God*. The following viewpoint is an excerpt from his *Know Why You Believe*.

Consider the following questions while reading:
1. **List and briefly explain some of the evidences Little offers to prove the existence of God.**
2. **What are the qualities of water which lead the author to refer to it as an additional proof for the existence of God?**

Taken from *Know Why You Believe,* by Paul E. Little. Revised edition © 1968 by Inter-Varsity Christian Fellowship of the USA and used by permission of Inter-Varsity Press.

There is in human existence no more profound question demanding an answer than "Is there a god?" The question must be answered by every human being, and the answer is far-reaching in its implications...

NO SCIENTIFIC PROOF

We must be clear from the outset that it is not possible to "prove" God in the scientific method sense of the word. But it can be said with equal emphasis that you can't "prove" Napoleon by the scientific method. The reason lies in the nature of history itself and in the limitations of the scientific method. In order for something to be "proved" by the scientific method, it must be repeatable. One cannot announce a new finding to the world on the basis of a single experiment. But history in its very nature is nonrepeatable. No one can "rerun" the beginning of the universe or bring Napoleon back or repeat the assassination of Lincoln or the crucifixion of Jesus Christ. But the fact that these events can't be "proved" by repetition does not disprove their reality as events...

ORDERLY UNIVERSE

If you can look about you and observe how intelligently PLANNED and executed is everything in nature and in plant and animal life — everything we see except the bungling, botching, polluting of God's beautiful handiwork by the clumsy hand of God-ignoring-and-rejecting MAN — and then say you doubt the existence of an All-wise, All-knowing, All-powerful Creator GOD, then I do not have much faith either in your thinking processes or your sincerity as a seeker of the TRUTH!

Herbert W. Armstrong, "God Does Exist," *Plain Truth*, June, 1972

What evidence is there for God? It is very significant that recent anthropological research has indicated that among the farthest and most remote primitive peoples, today, there is a universal belief in God. And in the earliest histories and legends of peoples all around the world the original concept was of one God, who was the Creator...

The vast majority of humanity, at all times and in all places, has believed in some kind of god or gods. Though this fact is not conclusive proof, by any means, we should keep it in mind as we attempt to answer the big question.

Then there is the law of cause and effect to consider. No effect can be produced without a cause. We as human beings, and the universe itself, are effects which must have had a cause. We come eventually to an uncaused cause, who is God.

A further development of this line of thought has to do with the clearly observable order and design in the universe. No one would think a wrist watch could come into being without an intelligent designer. How much more incredible is it to believe that the universe, in its infinite complexity, could have happened by chance? The human body, for instance, is an admittedly astounding and complex organism — a continual marvel of organization, design, and efficiency...

PROOFS FROM DESIGN

Evidences of this design are abundant. It is unlikely that a monkey in a print shop could set Lincoln's *Gettysburg Address* in type. If we found a copy of it we would conclude that an intelligent mind was the only possible explanation for the printing. It is likewise incredible that water, for instance, with all its qualities, could have just happened. Bernard Ramm, quoting L. J. Henderson, enumerates some of these properties:

"Water has a high specific heat. This means that chemical reactions within the (human) body will be kept rather stable. If water had a low specific heat we would 'boil over' with the least activity. If we raise the temperature of a solution by 10 degrees Centigrade we speed up the reaction by two. Without this particular property of water, life would hardly be possible. The ocean is the world's thermostat. It takes a large loss of heat for water to pass from liquid to ice, and for water to become steam quite an intake of energy is required. Hence the ocean is a cushion against the heat of the sun and the freezing blast of the winter. Unless the temperatures of the earth's surface were modulated by the ocean and kept within certain limits, life would either be cooked to death or frozen to death.

"Water is the universal solvent. It dissolves acids, bases and salts. Chemically, it is relatively inert, providing a medium for reactions without partaking in them. In the bloodstream it holds in solution the minimum of 64 substances. Perhaps if we knew the actual number it would be a staggering figure. Any other solvent would be a pure sludge! Without the peculiar properties of water, life as we know it would be impossible..."

The earth itself is evidence of design. "If it were much smaller an atmosphere would be impossible (e.g. Mercury and

67

Silent Summit

Artist: Jack Hamm. Reprinted with permission of Religious Drawings, Inc.

the moon); if much larger the atmosphere would contain free hydrogen (e.g. Jupiter and Saturn). Its distance from the sun is correct — even a small change would make it too hot or too cold. Our moon, probably responsible for the continents and ocean basins, is unique in our solar system and seems to have originated in a way quite different from the other relatively much smaller moons. The tilt of the [earth's] axis insures the seasons, and so on."

DuNouy says that "the chance formulations of a typical protein molecule made up of 3,000 atoms is of the order of one to 2.02×10^{231}, or practically nil. Even if the elements are shaken up at the speed of the vibration of light, it would take 10^{234} billions of years to get the protein molecule [needed] for life, and life on the earth is limited to about two billion years."

GENESIS 1 AND SCIENCE

In the light of all these things we can conclude with Ramm's statement: "Genesis 1 now stands in higher repute than it could ever have stood in the history of science up to this point. We now have means whereby we can point to a moment of time, or to an event or cluster of events in time, which dates our present known universe. According to the best available data, that is of the order of four to five billion years ago. A series of calculations converge on about the same order of time. We cannot with our present information force a verdict for creation from the scientists, though that is not to be considered an impossibility. Perhaps the day will come when we have enough evidence from physics, astronomy, and astrophysics to get such a verdict from the scientists. In the meantime we can maintain that Genesis 1 is not out of harmony with the trend of scientific information."

RECOGNIZING ETHNOCENTRIC STATEMENTS

Ethnocentrism is the attitude or tendency of people to view their race, religion, culture, group, or nation as superior to others, and to judge others on that basis. An American, whose custom is to eat with a fork or spoon, would be making an ethnocentric statement when saying, "The Chinese custom of eating with chopsticks is stupid."

Ethnocentrism has promoted much misunderstanding and conflict. It emphasizes cultural and religious differences and the notion that one's national institutions or group's customs are superior.

Ethnocentrism limits people's ability to be objective and to learn from others. Education in the truest sense stresses the similarities of the human condition throughout the world and the basic equality and dignity of all people.

Consider each of the following statements carefully. Mark *E* for any statement you think is ethnocentric. Mark *N* for any statement you think is not ethnocentric. Mark *U* if you are undecided about any statement.

E = Ethnocentric
N = Not Ethnocentric
U = Undecided

_____ 1. Christianity is spiritually superior to Oriental religions such as Buddhism and Hinduism.

_____ 2. The feminist movement in Western culture is engaged in the slow execution of Christ and Yahweh.

_____ 3. The belief in God is reactionary and harmful, standing forever in the way of betterment of the human condition.

_____ 4. In the final analysis, the message of Jesus is morally and ethically superior to that of Budda and Mohammed.

_____ 5. Christianity is certainly one of the world's major religions.

_____ 6. God has given many women gifts to pastor, administrate, teach, preach, counsel and lead.

_____ 7. The Jews are God's "chosen people."

_____ 8. All peoples are children of God.

_____ 9. "I am glad that I am a Christian. It offers me a spiritual satisfaction which no other religion has been able to do."

_____ 10. All religious revelation proves, on investigation, to be human, and generally fraudulent.

_____ 11. Belief in God is the best way we know for relating to the mystery and the paradox that lie at the very heart of life.

_____ 12. If any single factor can explain the superiority of Western culture, it is the unique influence of the Christian Church.

_____ 13. Although woman is subordinate in rank she is not inferior.

BIBLIOGRAPHY OF PERIODICAL ARTICLES

Mortimer Adler — *God Exists: No Doubt About It,* **U.S. Catholic,** October, 1980, p. 26

American Atheist — *Taking God Off the City Steps,* March, 1980, p. 10.

Herbert W. Armstrong — *Does God Exist?,* **Plain Truth,** June, 1972 p. 17.

Christian Science Monitor — *God Is Real,* September 8, 1973.

William F. Dankenbring — *Heaven, Hell and the Hereafter,* **Plain Truth,** July/August 1973, p. 24.

Theodore M. Hesburgh — *Will There Still Be a God?.* **Saturday Review/World,** August 24, 1974, p. 82.

Andrew T. LePeau — *Panic or Peace: The Challenge of Faith,* **HIS,** December, 1979, p. 27.

John McIntyre — *A Physicist Believes,* **Liberty,** March/April, 1979, p. 2.

William E. Moody — *Can We Prove God's Existence?,* **Christian Science Sentinel,** March 3, 1980, p. 355.

Kai Nielsen — *Does God Exist?: Reflections on Disbelief,* **Free Inquiry,** Spring, 1981, p. 21.

Michael L. Peterson — *Reid Debates Hume: Christian Versus Skeptic,* **Christianity Today,** September 22, 1978, p. 23.

Time — *Modernizing the Case for God,* April 7, 1980, p. 65.

Harvey Wheeler — *The Phenomenon of God,* **Center Magazine,** March/April, 1971, p. 7.

Joe L. Wheeler — *The Debate of the Century: Does God Really Exist?,* **Liberty,** January/February, 1977.

Chapter **3**

Religion and human experience

What Role Should Women Have in the Churches?

"Although woman is subordinate in rank she is not inferior."

Women Should Not Have Authority in the Church

David R. Nicholas

David R. Nicholas is Academic Dean at Southwestern Baptist College in Phoenix, Arizona. In his latest work, *What's a Woman to Do... In the Church?*, he turns to the authority of the Bible to illustrate the role women should play in the church. The following viewpoint is an excerpt from Nicholas' book.

Consider the following questions while reading:

1. **Nicholas offers two biblical indications that women were meant to be under the authority of men, what are they?**
2. **According to the author, what are some of the roles women can play in the church?**
3. **Do you agree with the author's arguments? Why or why not?**

The idea that God desires woman to be subordinate to her husband is rooted deep in both the Old and New Testaments. Now, some might quickly object to such a statement and say, "Wait a minute! Isn't this just an antiquated idea based upon an interpretation which reflects a male bias?" Well, I would be the first to admit that there was indeed a male bias, which was deeply ingrained in Roman, Greek and Jewish culture. Roman law, for example, provided that the husband was the sole and absolute head of his wife. His will was law, where she was concerned, and she had no appeal from his decisions. Similarly, in the Greek world Sophocles had said, "Silence confers grace upon a woman." In Greek culture a woman, unless she was very poor or loose morally, led a very secluded life...

In Jewish culture, a woman's lot was no better. Under Jewish law, a woman was a thing. She had no legal rights whatever. She was viewed as a possession of her husband just as much as his house, his flocks or other material goods...

Nevertheless, as will be discussed later, it was the influence of Christianity, and particularly the emphasis of the Apostle Paul, which helped to elevate women to a position of dignity and worth. Yet this elevation of women was not intended to invalidate the order which God has established for the church and the home relative to the biblical model of male leadership...

BIBLICAL AUTHORITY

Where are the indications that the woman was to be under the authority of the man? Well, the fact that man was created first and that woman originated from man is the first indication. The second is that it was Eve, who being deceived by Satan, fell into transgression. "Hold it," you protest, "doesn't the Bible say that both Adam and Eve disobeyed? Why should Eve take the rap? Does it matter which child takes the first cookie?" Now, before

MESSENGERS, NOT ADMINISTRATORS

In both the Old and New Testaments, we find that God did use some righteous women in the office of a prophetess. if we study these examples carefully, we will see that their function has often been misinterpreted and that their office carried no administrative authority, but that they were simply used of God to convey a message to one of His servants, or to other people — but NEVER in the capacity of preaching or exercising authority over them.

The Plain Truth, November, 1963

anyone accuses me of being an incorrigible chauvinist, let me hasten to point out that this is precisely how the Apostle Paul interprets the creation narrative in 1 Corinthians 11:7-9...

Writing under the inspiration of the Holy Spirit, the Apostle Paul states in 1 Corinthians 11:7-9.

For a man ought not to have his head covered since he is the image and glory of God; but the woman is the glory of man.

For man does not originate from woman, but woman from man; for indeed man was not created for the woman's sake, but woman for the man's sake...

I believe that the Apostle Paul is saying here that although woman is subordinate in rank, she is not inferior...

AUTHORITY FOR MEN

Sisters in Christ, do you want the blessing of God in ministry? Do you long to share in the work committed to the church? You can. Assuredly. But keep in mind the Bible pattern—God reserves authority for men. In all other places you can help as you are led.

George Sweeting, "Is The Church Unfair to Women?", *Moody*, March, 1980

GENESIS AND THE FALL

Now, we must turn our attention to the effects of the Fall upon the relationship between man and woman. In Genesis 3:13,16 we read:

The Lord God said to the woman, "what is this you have done?" And the woman said, "The serpent deceived me and I ate" (verse 13).

To the woman He said,
"I will greatly multiply your pain in childbirth,
In pain you shall bring forth children;
Yet your desire shall be for your husband,
And he shall rule over you" (verse 16)

With these words God initiated the curse upon the woman because of her role in the Fall. It should be observed as well, that man was also cursed because he listened to his wife and ate of the forbidden tree. The curse resulting from man's disobediance is recorded in Genesis 3: 17-19, and has to do primarily with the ground and the sentence upon man to eat bread by the sweat of his face (toil) and to do so until he returns to the dust from which he was formed (death)...

David R. Nicholas

A WOMAN CAN SERVE

While it is true that the sphere of woman's ministry does not include authoritative local church leadership, such as that of elder, pastor-teacher or deacon, there are numerous ministries in which women can and should be involved. As we study the New Testament we see women teach, pray, prophesy, perform diaconal tasks and minister in a variety of other ways. Since there is a heavy emphasis in the New Testament upon women performing diaconal service, it would appear that churches are at liberty to select women to serve as deaconesses. In this way dedicated Christian women can be of tremendous help to the deacons and to the church in general.

Think of the variety of ways dedicated women can serve in the church. Whether as deaconesses, or in some other capacity, they can serve as counselors to girls and women who respond to an invitation by going forward in a church service. They can assist pastors and deacons in visitation programs. They can call in hospitals and convalescent homes. They can help in the preparation of the Lord's supper (communion services). They can give spiritual encouragement to other women in the congregation during times of perplexity, hardship and spiritual decline. They can assist female baptismal candidates. They can supervise the delivery of flowers and the sending of cards to the shut-ins or bereaved. Many a faithful pastor thanks God for dedicated women who serve in so many ways, and by doing so strengthen their church's fellowship and testimony...

SUBORDINATE BUT ESSENTIAL

The Christian woman portrays Christlikeness, not inferiority, when she sumits to the will of God by patterning her role in the local church after the guidelines God has given us in His Word. Her role is subordinate, but nonetheless essential in the ministry of the church...

Let us pray that God will raise up an increasing number of women who are not only willing to utilize their gifts and abilities in the service of Christ, but who will also engage in the most powerful ministry of all—the ministry of prayer. The prayer ministry of a woman is strategically vital to her children, her husband and her church. As the book of James tells us, the effective prayer of the righteous can accomplish much (James 5:16b). I know. I have a mother who prays for me.

"God has given women gifts to pastor, administrate, teach, preach, counsel and lead the body of Christ."

Women Should Have Authority in the Church

Liz Emrey

Liz Emrey is Associate Pastor at the First Baptist Church, White Plains, New York. The following viewpoint was a speech delivered by Rev. Emrey to a group at the National American Baptist Churches offices in Valley Forge, Pennsylvania. Her remarks were prompted by the Study on the Community of Women and Men in the Church (SWIM) issued by the World Council of Churches.

Consider the following questions while reading:

1. List some of the specific examples the author gives related to bias against women as authority figures in the church.
2. Where does the author claim the call to church leadership comes from?
3. What did the author's mother mean when she said: "Better a prostitute, at least you wouldn't be sinning against your womanhood?"
4. Do you agree with Liz Emrey's arguments regarding women in the church? Why or why not?

Liz Emrey, "Can Women Have Authority in the Church?," *The Apple Core,* Volume V, Number 1, April, 1980. Reprinted with permission of the author.

Liz Emrey

I was asked to speak today on the problem of women and authority in the church. Women in our denomination have been officially encouraged to seek leadership roles in every area of the church. We were one of the first denominations to ordain women. Yet, as the SWIM report clearly shows, there is great resistance to women as ministers in our churches. This bias against women as leaders not only affects ordained women but all women who are called to positions of authority in the church.

THE WRONG IMAGE

In Southern California where I have lived for the last eight years many churches are restricting the deaconate to men. A choir director at one of our churches confided to me that in applying for an earlier church position, she had been told that she was more qualified that the other applicants, but they had chosen a man instead. The selection committee said that they preferred to have a man as leader. A woman did not project the proper authoritative image.

Unfortunately, this is not a regional problem. In my own church in New York several members of the congregation had great reservations about calling me to be their associate pastor. They frankly told me that they liked me and considered me to be amply qualified, but they just couldn't relate to a woman as an authority figure...

A CRIPPLED CHURCH

Unless we choose to withstand God, we must clear the way for all women to respond to the call of God as they experience it, for to deny them their calling is to condemn the church to limp into the kingdom of God on one leg.

Margaret Ann Cowden, *The American Baptist,* April, 1978

WE ARE ALL SERVANTS

Consciously or unconsciously many people have developed set roles for women and men in the church. Women are to be the servants, the helpers. Men are to be the leaders, the authority figures. This division between servants and leaders is not just a cultural bias, but a total misunderstanding of Christ's teachings on servanthood and authority in the church.

We are all called to be servants, one to another. Jesus washed his friend's dirty feet and told all of us to do likewise. No matter what work we do in the church our attitude should be that of humility, of servanthood. This is why our ministers are uncomfortable with clerical garb and Roman collars. Many of us dislike being called Reverend or Doctor. We believe that those signs of our office do not encourage people to confide in us, but set us apart from the very people we have been called to serve...

We are all called to be servants to one another, but we are not all called to be leaders in the church. Leadership depends on God choosing and empowering us and the recognition of our call by the community. Our authority to lead God's people comes primarily from God. It is not natural talents, educational background or

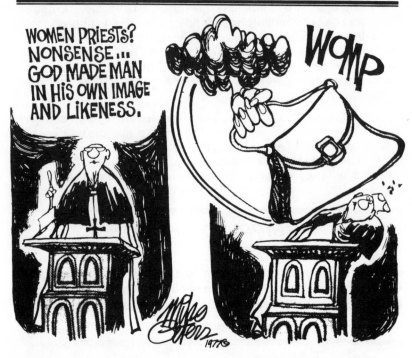

Artist: Mike Peters. Reprinted by permission of United Feature Syndicate, Inc.

the fatherly image someone may project that qualifies a person to exercise God's authority in the church. We are pastors, leaders, administrators, teachers because God has called us to the task. As for myself, I was not delighted by God's choice. I was raised as an Irish Catholic. When I mentioned to my mother that I was considering seminary, she half-jokingly said, "Better a prostitute, at least you wouldn't be sinning against your womanhood." I could not blame my mother. I was uncomfortable with women as leaders in the church. Each time I prayed, I tried to ignore God's persistent call to enter the ministry. I tried to use the Bible as my defense against God. But even Paul, that supposed male chauvinist, would not support me. In 1 Cor. 11:5 he cautions women to dress modestly, but does not in any way discourage them from leading prayer and prophesizing in the church. The only women he even tries to silence are those who are asking questions during the worship service. God slowly began to wear me down and convince me that the Lord would give me the gifts that would determine the paths of my ministry. It is our spiritual gifts that show each of us how we can serve, not our anatomy, our nationality or our social status. As Paul so unhesitatingly declared, "In Christ there is neither Jew nor Greek, there is neither slave nor free person, and no male nor female, for you are all one in Christ Jesus."

WHAT IS RIGHT?

If anything is right, the right of women to have the same opportunity as men is right. That should hold true in all our institutions: in business, the family, politics, the armed services, religion.

William Safire, *New York Times Service,* December, 1979

ONE SUFFERS, ALL SUFFER

God has given many women gifts to pastor, administrate, teach, preach, counsel and lead the Body of Christ. But these gifts are useless if we do not encourage women to recognize their particular calls to service. We as a denomination sin against God and ourselves when we discourage women from becoming ministers or leaders in the church. For as Paul said, "If one member suffers, the whole Body suffers."

Look around in our churches, in our Women's Guild. Where are our young women, our young families? Last year many young women came to me, a university chaplain, to tell me that they believed in equality for women and thus could no longer consider themselves Christians. One of our best graduates of the University of Redlands, a strong leader in the BYF and the First Baptist Church, is now a Methodist pastor. She told me that she felt called to the ministry and did not want to waste her time fighting for her right to serve in our denomination.

The women's liberation movement is not just my problem and that of women like myself, just as the acceptance of Greeks into the leadership of the church was not simply Paul's problem. The majority of American women between 25-65 are working for their living. Many are in leadership positions. They will not continue to accept subservient roles in the church. We need to affirm their gifts while being sensitive to the traditional biases against women as leaders in the church.

"The long history of the.. church has been that of a male priesthood — this tradition is not hastily or lightly to be broken."

Why Women Should Not Be Priests

David R. Stuart

David R. Stuart is a pseudonym for the Episcopal priest who wrote the following viewpoint. In the opening paragraph, the author states his reason for remaining anonymous. He then proceeds to offer several psychological, sociological and spiritual reasons why women should be excluded from the priesthood.

Consider the following questions while reading:
1. **Why has the author of this viewpoint chosen to remain anonymous?**
2. **The author claims that a pregnant or beautiful woman in a church pulpit would prove a great distraction to the congregation. Do you agree? Why or why not?**
3. **According to the author, why would a woman's role as "mother" conflict with her role as priest?**

From *The Ordination of Women: Pro and Con,* ed. M. P. Hamilton and N. S. Montgomery, © 1975 Morehouse-Barlow Co., Inc. Used by permission.

I have been asked to write on the nontheological objections to ordaining women and it was only after considerable reflection that I agreed to do so. The importance of the subject is obvious, for the beloved church which nurtures us and which we attempt to serve is in danger, in real danger, and this should constitute a clear call for us all to think and pray that we may be concerned actively for the church's spiritual welfare. On the other hand, the topic is dangerous, for anyone who ventures to speak out against a popular movement is in personal danger, the danger of being misunderstood and misrepresented, of losing one's privacy and the humility that is more easily maintained in quiet service rather than public debate. However, the cause of defending truth is a claim which overrides personal reluctance, if not individual anonymity.

While I agreed to let another speak on the theological reasons against the ordination of women to the priesthood I would like to say a word or two on that matter because it has bearing on the rest of my contribution. I am one who believes there are weighty theological reasons against women's ordination, sufficient and complementary to the case that I shall argue, but I am aware that they are not convincing to everyone. Part of the reason, I submit, is because neither the Jewish tradition, the biblical church nor the church of the first nineteen centuries was remotely interested in such a venture! They never discussed it theologically because it would have been preposterous of them to do so. If they had, I have no doubt they would have condemned it clearly and unequivocally, and upon such judgment we today would dismiss it.

The reason the church did not consider it in times past (and this is important to know) is that they knew in their bones that it would be wrong psychologically, sociologically, and spiritually...

PSYCHOLOGICAL

The argument from psychology is a delicate one. It touches on human pride, on feelings of inferiority and superiority; it conjures up sexual images which are confusing and which cannot be dealt with on a rational level alone for they raise deep issues of who we are and what God intended us to be...

Now the role of a priest is partly to be the representative of mankind (used generically) to God. Christ himself chose men to be apostles, the early church ordained men to be priests and consecrated men to be bishops. For generations the worshiper has heard the sounds of a male voice reading the prayers of consecration, for centuries the priest-confessor has been a man. Men were and continue to be the leaders, the initiators, the heads of households familial and ecclesiastical and it would be psychologically confusing as well as historically disruptive to substitute

86

A MALE MINISTRY

The word of God in Holy Scripture shows us a ministry that is predominately male. There are no exceptions in the Old Testament to the rule of a male priesthood, though women are shown there as prophets, seers and judges.

Bishop Stanley Atkins, *The Theological Case Against Women's Ordination*

women for that office. The long history of the Holy Catholic Church has been that of a male priesthood—this tradition is not hastily or lightly to be broken.

Reflect for a moment, putting aside those canons of good taste which normally and rightfully govern our thoughts regarding worship, how would you react to the appearance of a pregnant woman in the pulpit? Giving absolution? How would you, the reader—male or female—react to the sight of a beautiful long-haired woman celebrating the Eucharist? Attractive, yes, but also distracting. And I do not believe that the reverse is true, that a handsome male priest produces sexual distractions in the minds of women, for the dynamics of sexual attractiveness work differently for each sex. A handsome young male priest might well elicit feelings of admiration and even love in some women, but it would seldom be inclusive of the sexual phantasies which, for physiological and psychological reasons, occur in a man placed in a similar position vis-a-vis a woman...

SOCIOLOGICAL

The crucial question of role differentiation which is central in all cultures is essentially a product of physiological distinctions. In nearly all primitive cultures the male was the hunter, the woman the housekeeper. Both of them worked, indeed when one adds raising crops to the duties of women as occurred in some societies, women sometimes worked harder than their husbands who spent their time in discussion of government and the preparation and practice of religious rituals. The differentiation, however apportioned, was always there and it served deep psychic and societal purposes. It also served some very practical physical needs, for the women were the child bearers, and that social function which is of primary importance, not only gave them great status within their society, but also necessitated, because of its accompanying bodily inconveniences and occasional restrictions, a division and a sharing of tribal tasks not required of males.

Today we are a long way from primitive society, but we are still,

THE ATTITUDE OF CHRIST

Jesus Christ did not call any woman to become part of the Twelve. If he acted in this way, it was not in order to conform to the customs of his time, for his attitude towards women was quite different from that of his milieu, and he deliberately and courageously broke with it.

Pope Paul VI. Courtesy of Religious News Service Photo.

unless some highly dangerous biological tricks are perfected and foolishly adopted, in a situation where for nine months of each pregnancy the woman carries and nurtures one or more babies. And while definitive scientific studies have yet to be made, it is a likely hypothesis that it is the mother who is normally the best person to remain in that close personal proximity to an infant that will ensure its healthiest upbringing, until as a child it gains satisfaction from participating in group behavior. These responsibilities require considerable time away from other duties, and society, far from denying them, affords and encourages their appropriation. Do we really want to impose on married women the onerous, around-the-clock and around-the-year demands of a parish priest? I would argue that such a role is in conflict with the best interests of motherhood, probably with that of the baby, and often with that of the congregation...

The right to equal status is not the same as the right to similar roles and it is a sign of a sick society, if not a sick individual, that tries to achieve it.

There are some women who argue that all they want is the *right* to be ordained, even if they do not, themselves, wish to appropriate that right. I suggest this reveals a deep insecurity and feelings of inferiority which certainly deserve sensitive and careful attention...

ECCLESIASTICAL

Many women say they have been "called" to the priesthood and believe it is their God-given vocation. I do not doubt their personal talents nor their sincerity. However, unlike some denominations which permit any person "called" to be in effect self-ordained and to exercise his or her ministry according to individual whim, the Episcopal Church is part of the greater Catholic tradition which has always tested a "call" against the spirit-led wisdom of the larger church. There are many men who are both able and sincere and yet have not passed the necessary academic and psychological tests, have not gained Episcopal recognition of their call and hence have been refused ordination. Ordination to the priesthood in the Catholic Church is not and never has been a right, rather it has been a summons both by God *and* by his body on earth, the church. If we were to stray from Catholic and Orthodox tradition in such a central matter as the priesthood, some believe we will have lost the Apostolic validity of the orders we presently have, that the priesthood now given us will be cheapened, and all recognise it will greatly dim the hope of important ecumenical cooperation and progress...

There are deep mysteries in Christianity and feelings are as important as rationality when we seek to probe mysteries. Many of us *feel* a positive move for ordination at this time would be wrong. Do not dismiss us, have respect for our prayerful petitions — *festina lente.* There is heartfelt confusion and doubt among us—let us not be tempted to move to a position where schism becomes for many an option and for some a necessity. Rather respecting our honest differences and the historical, theological, ecumenical, psychological and social complexity of this matter, let us now say "no" to women's ordinations.

CHRIST'S WILL

Women cannot be ordained to the priesthood of Jesus Christ in the Church for the simple reason that its founder Jesus Christ, the Source of its teachings, of its graces, of its power, and of its authority, has not included this practice in the permanent Deposit of Faith which He confided to His Apostles, and which they left us both by living Tradition and in the inspired Scriptures.

Monsignor Arthur H. Durand, *The Wanderer,* December 9, 1978

"The rights of women denied and delayed is an injustice, an act of violence, a repudiation of the Gospel."

Why Women Should Be Priests

Harvey F. Egan

Harvey F. Egan is pastor of the Church of St. Joan of Arc, a Catholic parish in Minneapolis, Minnesota. St. Joan is a parish that emphasizes contemporary liturgies and the social implications of the Christian gospel. In the following viewpoint, Rev. Egan demonstrates a strong support for the total participation of women in the church. He expresses himself from a woman's point of view.

Consider the following questions while reading:

1. Do you agree with the author that the "women's movement is helping to renew the church and making it more humane and Christian?" Why or why not?
2. What kind of arguments does the author offer to support his position on women's equality in the church?

Harvey F. Egan, "It's Time for Churches To Expurge Sins of Sexism," *Minneapolis Star,* May 16, 1980. Reprinted with permission.

One man's suggestions for a creed of Christian feminists:

We are proud to be women. We are persons. We have personal rights. Many of our personal rights are being denied or violated in our society and church. We have been too timid in protesting the injustices that prevail against women. We now intend to insist on the recognition of and respect for our personal rights—with all deliberate speed.

The rights of women denied and delayed is an injustice, an act of violence, a repudiation of the Gospel. Discrimination based on sex is a sin. Sexism is unjust discrimination. Sexism is a sin. Sexism by a church adds scandal to the sin.

HISTORICAL MESSAGES

We who hope to remain with the Christian community and the congregation of our choice now resolve to meet frequently in order to become better informed and more effective in seeking justice for all women. We may thus enlarge and enhance a women's movement which is helping to renew the church, making it more humane and Christian.

CHALLENGE FOR THE '80s

Until the institutional Catholic church undertakes a serious, critical examination of its modes of acting toward women, it cannot, it will not, give witness to justice in the world. The challenge for women in the '80s is to confront and eradicate the systematic evils of sexism, clericalism, and paternalism.

Sister Theresa Kane, from an address to the Leadership Conference of Womens Religious

We will study history, searching for positive messages and inspirations. We will, however, concentrate on finding and following the insights and recommendations of contemporary heroines. We recently came out of the kitchen and went back to school; now we are moving out of the library and into the marketplace.

Respect for the rights of women in the churches will be assured as increasing justice is won for women in our total society—in social, economic, educational, political and domestic experiences. We are dedicated to work for full justice in all these areas. We are not inclined to perpetuate a pink-collar ghetto in our society.

We totally support the ERA. We await the public endorsement and enthusiastic support of the ERA by the lagging leaders of most churches in the United States. For more than a century, our churches were slow to protest one form of slavery. Another form of slavery continues. Another emancipation declaration is long overdue. Will tardiness become the fifth mark of the church?

Artist: Mike Peters. Reprinted by permission of United Feature Syndicate, Inc.

MEN CAN HELP

Within the women's movement, we will listen to and welcome the support of men who understand our anguish and the urgency of our cause. Tomorrow many more men will be liberated from their own form of servitude, a jaundiced male mystique, and assist the struggle for universal justice. We aim at justice for all the members of the human family; the liberation of women is an essential part of that goal and struggle.

We deplore sexist language, including the plethora of praise gushed forth in religious rites to the alleged superiority of males. We applaud persons striving to screen out sexist language from liturgies and design new religious symbols which will reflect our needs and hopes.

We tend to think of God as "the One who is the Matrix of all Being, the source of both all that is said and all that might be, the font of life and the renewal of life in new and redeeming patterns.

93

This great Matrix is neither male nor female, the foundation of the authentic personhood of both men and women." (Rosemary Ruether, "Christianity and Crisis," Dec. 10, 1979.) For persons who think of God in more personal terms, both feminine and masculine images may be helpful. Many of us have found God in ourselves and we love her powerfully.

The women's movement includes several struggles, but also harbors some many-splendored experiences. We will not focus exclusively on a single issue. We will, through listening, studying, praying and taking action, become well-informed on all the important issues of our society because every issue has immense applications for all women.

TOTAL PARTICIPATION

We will become energetic and effective in the reform or replacement of anachronistic organizations with ingrained sexist patterns—the rigid political parties, business institutions, unions, schools and churches.

We intend to participate as fully as possible in the life of the church: in its sacramental and liturgical life; in its educational and social action programs; and in its administration and leadership. We cannot, however, give any assurance that we will remain subservient in a religious institution dominated by males. There are nearly 400 million Catholic women throughout the world, and we are all ecclesiastically and exclusively directed by a basilica full of males.

Clerical gesturing, without our rightful participation in the life of the church, is intolerable paternalism. We are determined to rescue our church from benign neglect, seeking to create an awareness of the problem and an eagerness for the solution by massive marches, stubborn sit-ins, heroic works of mercy, silent treatments, loud wailings, whatever may be necessary. We now earnestly work for, but will not indefinitely wait for, significant changes and justice for women in the church. We may raise a little hell before we get to heaven.

We will search and work for a Christian community beyond sexism. We seek a theology, spirituality and liturgy for all Christians—not certain formulas for men and other formulas for women.

A NEW BEGINNING

A few of us aspire to the Catholic priesthood, but only to a renewed and improved priesthood which respects a person's right to choose marriage or celibacy. We are convinced there are no physical, psychological, scriptural or theological reasons why

A MATTER OF FREEDOM

Human beings have the right to choose freely the state of life which they prefer, and therefore the right to establish a family, with equal rights and duties for man and woman, and also the right to follow a vocation to the priesthood or the religious life.

Pope John XXIII

a woman could not be ordained. There are only institutional barriers reflecting the sexism of our society; these artificial and outrageous obstacles can and must be overcome.

If only one woman wishes to be ordained all of us are dedicated to work so that her right may be respected and her vocation followed. When an official welcome is given by the Catholic Church for qualified women to be ordained and engage in an effective ministry, the acute Catholic vocation shortage will be alleviated.

We hope Catholic women who wish to be ordained and their friends will gather frequently for the offering of a Eucharistic prayer.

The women's movement is a leaven in the loaf of humanity and Christianity. The bread is rising—and we pledge ourselves to work earnestly so that, in a justice-respecting society and church, all persons may be nourished and give nourishment in love.

"All of the roles that men and women have been taught to consider as God-given will be reevaluated... Society itself will be transformed to the point that it will no longer be a patriarchy."

Women Priests Will Transform Society

Naomi R. Goldenberg

Naomi R. Goldenberg is a noted psychologist of religion and a feminist theologian. *Publishers Weekly* called her recent book, *Changing of the Gods,* "a challenging controversial view of the stirrings of religious feminism." In the following viewpoint, an excerpt from her book, the author makes this far-reaching assertion: Religious feminism will innitiate a radical transformation not only of western religion, but also of western society.

Consider the following questions while reading:
1. **What arguments did Pope Paul VI offer to support the Vatican's ban on allowing women into the priesthood?**
2. **What changes in church and society does the author see occuring in the next four decades as a result of the increasing prominence of women in religious life?**
3. **Do you feel that these changes would be good for church and society? Why or why not?**

The feminist movement in Western culture is engaged in the slow execution of Christ and Yahweh. Yet very few of the women and men now working for sexual equality within Christianity and Judaism realize the extent of their heresy.

Within Christianity, devout Catholic and Protestant women are rewriting liturgies to refer to "sisters" as well as to "brothers," calling attention to the importance of women in the story of Christ and seeking ordination as ministers and priests in greater numbers than ever before. Within Judaism, loyal Jewish women are improvising ceremonies to celebrate the birth of daughters as well as sons, establishing the right of females to be included in the *minyan** and founding publications that challenge the inferior position of women in the Jewish religion.

REFORMING TRADITIONS

The Jewish and Christian women who are reforming their traditions do not see such reforms as challenging the basic nature of Christianity and Judaism. Instead, they understand themselves to be improving the practice of their religions by encouraging women to share the responsibilities of worship equally with men.

As a psychologist of religion, I do not agree that improving the position of women is a minor alteration in Judaeo-Christian doctrine. The reforms that Christian and Jewish women are proposing are major departures from tradition. When feminists succeed in changing the position of women in Christianity and Judaism, they will shake these religions at their roots. The nature of a religion lies in the nature of the symbols and images it exalts in ritual and doctrine. It is the psychic picture of Christ and Yahweh that inspires the loves, the hates and the behavior patterns of Christians and Jews. The psychology of the Jewish and Christian religions depends on the masculine image that these religions have of their God. Feminists change the major psychological impact of Judaism and Christianity when they recognize women as religious leaders and as images of divinity.

THE WISDOM OF POPE PAUL

Conservative leaders of contemporary religious institutions understand that allowing women access to top positions of authority threatens the age-old composition of the institutions themselves.

In January 1977, Pope Paul VI issued a declaration affirming the Vatican's ban on allowing women to be ordained as Catholic priests. The document states that because Christ was a man and because he chose only male disciples, women can never serve as chief officials in the Catholic hierarchy.

Pope Paul used an impressive knowledge of how image and symbol operate in the human mind to build his case against female priests. "The priest," he explained, "is a sign ... a sign that must be perceptible and which the faithful must be able to recognize with ease. The whole sacramental economy is in fact based upon natural signs, on symbols imprinted upon the human psychology..."

Pope Paul reasoned that because the priest must represent Christ, i.e., God, the priest must resemble God. If the priest looked very different from Christ, a follower would not feel immediate connection between God and the priest who was supposed to embody *Him*. The Pope realized that people experience God through *His* representatives. If one were to change the sex of God's representatives, one would be changing the nature of God *Himself*. As the chief guardian of the Catholic faith, the Pope understood that he could not allow any serious tampering with the image of God...

TRANSFORMATION OF SOCIETY

The women's movement will bring about religious changes on a massive scale. These changes will not be restricted to small numbers of individuals practicing nonsexist religions within a sexist society. Society itself will be transformed to the point that it will no longer be a patriarchy. For if men are no longer supreme rulers on earth, how could one expect them to retain sovereignty in heaven?...

Naomi R. Goldenberg

CHANGE IS INEVITABLE

At the present moment, no major Christian denomination has more than a few token women in top authority positions. However, this exclusion is short-lived. In a few more decades, sizable numbers of women ministers will graduate from Protestant seminaries and will take charge of parishes throughout the Western world. Liberal Catholics will eventually win their fight to have women ordained as priests. The recognition of large numbers of women as Christian spiritual leaders will advance the personal dignity and social privilege of females everywhere.

However, we must ask ourselves what will happen to Christianity when women do succeed in changing traditions so that they are treated as the equals of men. Will not this major departure from the Christian view of women radically alter the religion? Pope Paul knew it would. The Pope understood that representatives of

Christianity mirror the image of God by calling to mind the male figure of Jesus Christ. If women play at being priests, they would play at being God; and Christianity, he insisted, can only afford to have men in that role...

NEW GODS ARE COMING

Judaism and Christianity have never been challenged to the extent that they will be in the next decades. The images of Christ and Yahweh will be questioned because of the very basic quality of maleness. All of the roles that men and women have been taught to consider as God-given will be re-evaluated. Although it is certainly true that small groups of Christians and Jews have departed from tradition by conceiving of God in female terms and by experimenting with new roles for men and women, such sects have been rather small-scale religious anomalies. The women's movement will bring about religious changes on a massive scale. These changes will not be restricted to small numbers of individuals practicing nonsexist religions within a sexist society. Society itself will be transformed to the point that it will no longer be a patriarchy. For if men are no longer supreme rulers on earth, how could one expect them to retain sovereignty in heaven?...

New gods will be born. Since "gods" always reflect the styles of behavior we see as possible, as our range of the possible expands so must our pantheon.

Up until recently, the only kind of legitimate public authority most of us could imagine was that of an adult male. As long as this image held us, we could picture God only as an old man. Now a growing number of us are able to imagine authority in new guises. Feminism is pushing us into an age of experimentation with new personifications of authority. We can picture public power held by a woman or group of women, shared by both sexes or rotated between the sexes. These more fluid concepts of hierarchy are certain to affect our view of God.

UNDERSTANDING STEREOTYPES

A stereotype is an oversimplified or exaggerated description of people or things. Stereotyping can be favorable. However, most stereotyping tends to be highly uncomplimentary and, at times, degrading.

Stereotyping grows out of our prejudices. When we stereotype someone, we are prejudging him or her. Consider the following example. It is part of an actual interview which appeared in a book by Gordon Allport, *The Nature of Prejudice:*

> *Mr. X:* The trouble with the Jews is that they only take care of their own group.
>
> *Mr. Y:* But the record of the Community Chest campaign shows that they gave more generously, in proportion to their numbers, to the general charities of the community, than do non-Jews.
>
> *Mr. X:* That shows they are always trying to buy favor and intrude into Christian affairs. They think of nothing but money; that is why there are so many Jewish bankers.
>
> *Mr. Y:* But a recent study shows that the percentage of Jews in the banking business is negligible, far smaller than the percentage of non-Jews.
>
> *Mr. X:* That's just it; they don't go in for respectable business; they are only in the movie business or run night clubs.

Notice how Mr. X, even when shown to be wrong, rigidly maintains an anti-Jewish bias. Why does he do this? Simply because he holds a negative prejudice directed toward Jews and will, when it is necessary, construct stereotypes which are consistent with his prejudice.

Read through the following list carefully. Mark *S* for any statement that is an example of stereotyping. Mark *N* for any statement that is not an example of stereotyping. Mark *U* if you are undecided about any statement. Then discuss and compare your decisions with other class members.

S = Stereotype
N = Not a stereotype
U = Undecided

_____ 1. Women priests and ministers would pay more attention to family affairs — children, finances, etc. — than to the spiritual concerns of their congregation.

_____ 2. Generally speaking, a religious person is more trustworthy than a non-religious person.

_____ 3. Atheists can be as moral and ethical as those who believe in God.

_____ 4. As a rule, intellectuals tend to disbelieve in the existence of God.

_____ 5. Emotionally, some people would be better off without religion.

_____ 6. It may be suspected that the wide appeal which Christianity has had has, in part, been due to the fact that the central figure constitutes a father-image of love, a God of love.

_____ 7. Catholics tend to be more tolerant than Protestants in their relationships with non-Christians.

_____ 8. In no field of human knowledge, not even religion, are there fixed truths.

_____ 9. Man has something more than animal instinct—the power of reason.

_____ 10. All superstitions, whether labeled "religion" or belonging to the "broken-mirror" class, start as a mere imaginary explanation for something not understood, and that is all they are.

_____ 11. Religion serves in many ways to impede the development of flexible thinking processes. This ultimately results in adult thinking that is rigid, confined and stereotyped.

_____ 12. As people grow nearer to their time of death (the elderly and terminally ill), they become more religious.

BIBLIOGRAPHY OF PERIODICAL ARTICLES

T. Beeson — *We Asked for Bread; You Have Given Us a Stone,* **The Christian Century,** December 6, 1978, p. 1172.

Christianity Today — *Canadians Take Radical Middle Ground Stand on Women's Issue,* July 18, 1980, p. 64.

J. Clemons and D. Hunt — *Support for Women Considering Ministry,* **The Christian Century,** May 23, 1979, p. 592.

John R. Donahue — *Women, Priesthood and the Vatican,* **America,** April 2, 1977, p. 285.

Doris Gottemoeller — *Women and Leadership in the Church: Problems and Promise,* **New Catholic World,** September/October 1980, p. 201.

Carter Heyward and Suzanne R. Hiatt — *The Trivialization of Women,* **Christianity and Crisis,** June 26, 1978, p. 158.

Paul King Jewett — *Why I Favor the Ordination of Women,* **Christianity Today,** June 6, 1975, p. 7.

Jane Marie Luecke — *The Dominance Syndrome,* **The Christian Century,** April 27, 1977, p. 405.

J.C. Lyles — *UMC's Women Clergy: Sisterhood and Survival,* **The Christian Century,** February 7, 1979, p. 117.

Berkeley and Alvera Mickelsen — *Does Male Dominance Tarnish Our Translations?,* **Christianity Today,** October 5, 1979, p. 23.

Brain A. Nelson — *Women Are also Called,* **The American Baptist,** September, 1978.

Michael Novak — *On the Ordination of Women,* **Commonwealth,** July 8, 1977, p. 425.

J.D. Quinn — *New ˙Testament Data on Priestly Ordination,* **America,** August 30- September 6, 1980. p. 94.

G. Lloyd Rediger — *The Feminine Mystique and the Ministry,* **The Christian Century,** July 4-11, 1979, p. 699.

Rosemary Radford Ruether — *Goddesses and Witches: Liberation and Countercultural Feminism,* **The Christian Century,** September 10-17, 1980, p. 842.

Rosemary Radford Ruether — *Why Males Fear Women Priests,* **The Witness,** July, 1980, p. 19.

Leonard Swidler — *Jesus Had Feminine Qualities, Too,* **National Catholic Reporter,** April 1, 1977, p. 15.

E.M. Tetlow — *Women in Ministry: A New Testament Perspective,* **America,** February 23, 1980, p. 138.

Chapter **4**

Religion and human experience

Has Organized Religion Helped or Harmed Society ?

"Religion has never made man free. It has never made man moral, temperate, industrious and honest."

Religion Is Slavery

Robert G. Ingersoll

Henry Ward Beecher acclaimed Robert G. Ingersoll (1833-1899) the "most brilliant speaker of the English tongue of all the men of the globe." Ingersoll devoted much of his oratorical talents to attacking religion and belief in God. Known as "the great agnostic," some of his more famous antireligious lectures included: "The Gods," "Some Mistakes of Moses," "Why I Am an Agnostic" and "Superstition." Ironically, he was the son of a devout Congregational minister. The following viewpoint is an excerpt from Ingersoll's last public address, "What Is Religion?"

Consider the following questions while reading:

1. Why does the author think religion has failed? List some of the things which he claims religion has failed to do.
2. What does the author suggest in place of religion?
3. Do you agree or disagree with the author's attack on religion? Why?

Robert G. Ingersoll, *What Is Religion?* A public address delivered in Boston on June 2, 1899.

Man has deceived himself. Nature is a mirror in which man sees his own image, and all supernatural religions rest on the pretence that the image, which appears to be behind this mirror, has been caught.

All the metaphysicians of the spiritual type, from Plato to Swedenborg, have manufactured their facts, and all founders of religion have done the same.

Suppose that an infinite God exists, what can we do for him? Being infinite, he is conditionless, he cannot be benefitted or injured. He cannot want. He has.

Think of the egotism of a man who believes that an infinite being wants his praise!

What has our religion done? Of course, it is admitted by Christians that all other religions are false, and consequently we need examine only our own. Has Christianity done good? Has it made men nobler, more merciful, nearer honest? When the Church had control, were men made better and happier?...

THE CRUELTY OF RELIGION

It cannot be denied there has been too much intolerance and illiberality entertained by the adherents of all systems of religion towards all opposing systems, and this spirit, carried to excess, has led to the most cruel tortures and deaths, the most bloody and devastating wars the world has known.

D.M. Bennett, *World's Sages, Thinkers and Reformers*

THE FAILURE OF RELIGION

Religion has been tried, and in all countries, in all times, has failed. Religion has never made men merciful. Remember the Inquisition. What effect did religion have on slavery? Religion has always been the enemy of science, of investigation and thought. Religion has never made man free: It has never made man moral, temperate, industrious and honest.

Are Christians more temperate, nearer virtue, nearer honesty than savages? Among savages do we not find that their vices and cruelties are the fruits of their superstitions?

To those who believe in the Uniformity of Nature, religion is impossible.

Can we affect the nature and qualities of substance by prayer?

Can we hasten or delay the tides by worship? Can we change winds by sacrifice? Will kneeling give us wealth? Can we cure disease by supplication? Can we add to our knowledge by ceremony? Can we receive virtue or honor as alms? Are not the facts in the mental world just as stubborn — just as necessarily produced — as the facts in the material world? Is not what we call mind just as natural as what we call body?

Religion rests on the idea that Nature has a master and that this master will listen to prayer; that this master punishes and rewards; that he loves praise and flattery and hates the brave and free.

Has man obtained any help from heaven?...

For thousands of years men and women have been trying to reform the world. They have created gods and devils, heavens and hells; they have written sacred books, performed miracles, built cathedrals and dungeons; they have crowned and uncrowned kings and queens; they have tortured and imprisoned, flayed alive and burned; they have preached and prayed; they have tried promises and threats; they have coaxed and persuaded; they have preached and taught, and in countless ways have endeavored to make people honest, temperate, industrious and virtuous; they have built hospitals and asylums, universities and schools, and seem to have done their very best to make mankind better and happier, and yet they have not succeeded...

ETHICS WITHOUT GOD

It is possible for human beings to lead meaningfull and wholesome lives for themselves and in service to their fellow human beings without the need of religious commandments or the benefit of clergy.

Paul Kurtz, "A Secular Humanist Declaration," *Free Inquiry,* Winter 1981

REASON—NOT RELIGION

Ignorance, poverty and vice must stop populating the world. This cannot be done by moral suasion. This cannot be done by talk or example. This cannot be done by religion or by law, by priest or by hangman. This cannot be done by force, physical or moral...

I look forward to the time when men and women by reason of their knowledge of consequences, of the morality born of intelligence, will refuse to perpetuate disease and pain, will refuse to fill the world with failures. Religion can never reform mankind because religion is slavery.

History Lesson

Artist: Kirby. Reprinted with permission of *The American Atheist.*

"Every great awakening of the church has been followed by great social advance."

Churches Improve Society

Donald McGavran

Donald McGavran is senior professor of mission at Fuller Seminary, Pasadena, California. Like most defenders of religion, McGavran is convinced that the world would still be in a state of moral barbarism were it not for the efforts of institutional churches. In the following viewpoint, he offers several specific examples in support of his conviction.

Consider the following questions while reading:

1. Why does the author think churches improve society?
2. What role have churches had in combating imperialism and racism?
3. How do churches promote social advances?
4. Do you think the author of this viewpoint is correct?

It is often suggested that there are better ways of improving society than through the influence of the church. But the fact is that wherever the church is firmly planted, life becomes more honest, more just, more humane, and more reasonable. Darkness recedes; righteousness flourishes. Communities become happier places in which to live. This is necessarily so, because the church is the Body of Christ. The church's standard of goodness is not imposed on it by the culture, nor is it a human construction, but rather it is an absolute standard of the Lord.

CHURCHES IMPROVE SOCIETY

The church improves society. When Eskimos—became Christians, the first thing they did was to stop killing off their aged parents. When certain tribes of Zaire became Christians, they ended constant warring against their neighbors. As communities on the American frontier became Christians, they began schools and colleges.

IMPERIALISM

Much of the attack on the church today is because it has not yet solved social evils that until recently were not even recognized as evil, imperialism—the rule of the weak by the powerful—was the principle according to which hundreds of Indian kingdoms rose and fell over the millenia. England's rule was simply one more in the sequence. Only recently has imperialism been recognized by the West as an evil. Only where the church is strong is the basic question ever raised as to whether it is pleasing to God for strong foreigners to rule weak nations.

HISTORIANS RESPECT RELIGION

Even the skeptical historian develops a humble respect for religion, since he sees it functioning and seemingly indispensable, in every land and age. To the unhappy, the suffering, the bereaved, the old, it has brought supernatural comforts valued by millions of souls as more precious than any natural aid. It has helped parents and teachers to discipline the young. It has conferred meaning and dignity upon the lowliest existence, and through its sacraments has made for stability by transforming human covenants into solemn relationships with God.

Will and Ariel Durant, *The Lessons of History*

RACISM

Racism also was just a fact of life. The Normans conquered the Saxons in 1066 and for a couple of hundred years Saxons were called "Saxon swine." Their girls were fair game for any Norman soldier. The caste system of Hinduism legalized and sanctified race prejudice. Despite a few minor adjustments, the caste system still rules India. Of every ten thousand marriages, only three are across caste lines. In most castes, anyone marrying outside the caste is promptly ostracized and declared dead.

The church recognizes racism as a sin and is warring against it. This is cause for rejoicing. Only slovenly provincial thinkers would castigate the church for what it is doing. It could be doing more, of course; who couldn't? But that it is doing anything is a miracle...

SOCIAL ADVANCES

I write forthrightly because many Christians, and I myself on occasion, find it easy to castigate the church for its failures and to minimize its successes. It would take too long to recount the social advances that the last hundred years have seen: the end of slavery, the institution in nation after nation of universal education, the end of European empires, the spreading of convictions concerning the rights of common men, the spread of a humane system of punishment, the recognition of the rights of women, children, and racial minorities, and on and on.

When you compare the lot of the darkskinned citizens of Brazil with the darkskinned of the United States, you see that in the states the racially disadvantaged have a substantial number of educated able men and women openly pleading their cause and fighting their battles, though in Brazil the dark-skinned have few educated advocates. Why? Churches in the states since 1865 have carried out two great redemptive actions. First, in scores of institutes and colleges they made education available to multitudes of freed slaves. It is easy to scorn this and say it was too little; but it was much more than was done in Brazil for the racially oppressed. Second, since 1865 the churches among the freed slaves have multiplied and have formed themselves into large denominations whose ministers have become powerful spokesmen for their people...

Every great awakening of the church has been followed by great social advance. The Wesleyan revival not only multiplied churches and spread believers around the globe, but it multiplied social conscience and opened millions of believers to God's radiant sunshine. In that clear light they saw that child labor in the mines was abhorrent to God. They discerned that drunkenness was against God's will. They freed slaves. They rejoiced in honest

110

rights and measures. Multiplication of churches necessarily means multiplication of godly convictions about how we—under today's circumstances with today's resources—are to love our neighbors as ourselves.

IT SHALL EVER BE

Artist: Jack Hamm. Reprinted with permission of Religious Drawings, Inc.

"Religion is, on almost every conceivable count, directly opposed to the goals of mental health."

Religion Is Neurosis

Albert Ellis

Albert Ellis, who received his Ph.D. from Columbia University in 1947, is a clinical psychologist of national stature. A prolific author, Dr. Ellis' reputation rest largely, but not solely, upon his studies in the area of sexual psychology. His books include: *The Case for Sexual Liberty, The Search for Sexual Enjoyment, Homosexuality* and *A New Guide to Rational Living.* In the following viewpoint, he draws upon his experience as a practicing psychologist to illustrate why he believes that religion is not conducive to sound mental health.

Consider the following questions while reading:

1. **List the nine personality traits which the author believes are important signs of good mental health.**
2. **Select five traits from your list and, using the author's arguments, show how religion harms personality development in these five areas.**
3. **Select one of the nine traits and attempt to defend the influence of religion on that trait.**

Albert Ellis, *The Case Against Religion: A Psychotherapist's View.* Published by the Society of Separationists, Inc., and reprinted with permission.

If religion is defined as man's dependence on a power above and beyond the human, then, as a psychotherapist, I find it to be exceptionally pernicious. For the psycho-therapist is normally dedicated to helping human beings in general and his patients in particular to achieve certain goals of mental health, and virtually all these goals are antithetical to a truly religious viewpoint.

Let us look at the main psychotherapeutic goals. On the basis of twenty years of clinical experience, and in basic agreement with most of my professional colleagues. I would say that the psychotherapist tries to help his patients to be minimally anxious and hostile; and to this end, he tries to help them to acquire the following kind of personality traits:

1. Self-interest
2. Self-direction
3. Tolerance
4. Acceptance of uncertainty
5. Flexibility
6. Scientific thinking
7. Commitment
8. Risk-taking
9. Self acceptance

These, then, are the kinds of personality traits which a psychotherapist is interested in helping his patients achieve and which he is also interested in fostering in the lives of millions who will never be his patients.

RELIGION AND MENTAL HEALTH

Now, does religion — by which, again, I mean faith unfounded on fact, or dependence on some supernatural deity — help human beings to achieve these healthy traits and thereby to avoid becoming anxious, depressed, and hostile?

The answer, of course, is that it doesn't help at all; and in most respects it seriously sabotages mental health. For religion, first of all, is not **self-interest;** it is god-interest.

The religious person must, by virtual definition, be so concerned with whether or not his hypothesized god loves him, and whether he is doing the right thing to continue to keep in this god's good graces, that he must, at very best, put himself second and must sacrifice some of his most cherished interests to appease this god. If, moreover, he is a member of any organized religion, then he must choose his god's precepts first, those of his church and its clergy second, and his own views and preferences third.

In a sense, the religious person must have no real views of his own; and it is presumptuous of him, in fact, to have any. In regard to sex-love affairs, to marriage and family relations, to business, to politics, and to virtually everything else that is important in his life, he must try to discover what his god and his clergy would like him to do; and he must primarily do their bidding...

In regard to **self-direction,** it can easily be seen from what has just been said that the religious person is by necessity dependent and other-directed rather than independent and self-directed...

Church Of The Weak Knees

Artist: Kirby. Reprinted with permission of *The American Atheist.*

Tolerance, again, is a trait that the firm religionist cannot possibly possess. "I am the Lord thy God and thou shalt have no other Gods before me," sayeth Jehovah. Which means, in plain English, that whatever any given god and his clergy believe must be absolutely, positively true; and whatever any other person or group believes must be absolutely, positively false...

If one of the requisites for emotional health is **acceptance of uncertainty,** then religion is obviously the unhealthiest state imaginable: since its prime reason for being is to enable the religionist to believe in a mystical certainty.

Just because life is so uncertain, and because millions of people think that they cannot take its vicissitudes, they invent absolutistic gods, and thereby pretend that there is some final, invariant answer to things. Patently, these people are fooling themselves — and instead of healthfully admitting that they do not need certainty, but can live comfortable in this often disorderly world, they stubbornly protect their neurotic-beliefs by insisting that there must be the kind of certainty that they foolishly believe that they need...

The trait of **flexibility,** which is so essential to proper emotional functioning, is also blocked and sabotaged by religious belief. For the person who dogmatically believes in god, and who sustains this belief with a faith unfounded in fact, which a true religionist of course must, clearly is not open to change and is necessarily bigoted...

In regard to **scientific thinking,** it practically goes without saying that this kind of cerebration is quite antithetical to religiosity. The main canon of the scientific method — as Ayer (1947), Carnap (1953), Reichenbach (1953) and a host of other modern philosophers of science have pointed out — is that, at least in some final analysis, or in principle, all theories be confirmable by some form of human experience, some empirical referent. But all religions which are worthy of the name contend that their superhuman entities cannot be seen, heard, smelled, tasted, felt, or otherwise humanly experienced, and that their gods and their principles are therefore distinctly beyond science...

COMMITMENT: GOOD AND BAD

In regard to the trait of **commitment,** the religious individual may — for once! — have some advantages. For if he is truly religious, he is seriously committed to his god, his church, or his creed; and to some extent, at least, he thereby acquires a major interest in life.

RELIGION AND RIGID THINKING

Religion serves in many ways to impede the development of flexible thinking processes. This ultimately results in adult thinking that is rigid, confined and stereotyped.

Eli S. Chesen, *Religion May Be Hazardous To Your Health*

Religious commitment also frequently has its serious disadvantages: since it tends to be obsessive-compulsive; and it may well interfere with other kinds of healthy commitments — such as deep involvements in sex-love relations, in scientific pursuits, and even in artistic endeavors. Moreover, it is a commitment that is often motivated by guilt or hostility, and may serve as a frenzied covering-up mechanism which masks, but does not really eliminate, these underlying disturbed feelings. It is also the kind of commitment that is based on falsehoods and illusions, and that therefore easily can be shattered, thus plunging the previously committed individual into the depths of disillusionment and despair...

In regard to **risk-taking,** it should be obvious that the religious person is highly determined not to be adventurous nor to take any of life's normal risks. He strongly believes in unvalidateable assumptions precisely because he does not want to risk following his own preferences and aims, but wants the guarantee that some higher power will back him...

Finally, in regard to **self-acceptance,** it should again be clear that the religious devotee cannot possibly accept himself just because he is alive, because he exists and has, by mere virtue of his aliveness, some power to enjoy himself. Rather, he must make his self-acceptance utterly contingent on the acceptance of his definitional god, the church and clergy who also serve this god, and all other true believers in his religion...

RELIGION IS NEUROSIS

If we summarize what we have just been saying, the conclusion seems inescapable that religion, is, on almost every conceivable count, directly opposed to the goals of mental health — since it basically consists of masochism, other-directedness, intolerance, refusal to accept uncertainty, unscientific thinking, needless inhibition, and self-abasement.

In the final analysis, then religion is neurosis. This is why I remarked, at a symposium on sin and psycho-therapy held by the American Psychological Association a few years ago, that from a mental health standpoint Voltaire's famous dictum should be reversed: for if there were a God, it would be necessary to uninvent Him.

"Religion . . . is an instrument in man's search for his identity."

Religion Improves Life

Henryk Skolimowski

In 1976, several professors at the University of Michigan were asked "to prepare a lecture as if it were the last lecture they would ever give." They were to emphasize those things which they felt "would be most important to say." Professor Henryk Skolimowski, of the Department of Philosophy, answered the call by presenting a lecture entitled "Life Will Prevail." In the following viewpoint, an excerpt from his lecture, Professor Skolimowski outlines the significance of religion in humankind's quest for identity.

Consider the following questions while reading:

1. **According to the author, what positive functions do traditional religions serve?**
2. **What does the author mean when he says, "Do not be overly impressed by the secondary aspects of religion?"**
3. **Do you agree with the author's thesis, namely, that religion has helped humankind "attain and preserve humanity?" Explain your answer.**

Henryk Skolimowski, "The Last Lecture ... Life Will Prevail," *Vital Speeches of the Day*, January 1, 1977. Reprinted with permission of the publisher.

We must once again look carefully at the structure and function of traditional religions. For religions were not merely institutionalized forms of spiritual tyranny, not merely an expression of our submission to omnipotent deities, but something much more vital, much more subtle, much more necessary.

RELIGIONS ARTICULATE IDEAS

Traditional religions have articulated the structures of man's need for worshiping ideals which are larger than man himself. These structures are often mystified and frequently distorted by practice and ritual. These distortions and mystifications should not obscure from our view the fact, however, that the primary function of religious structures is to provide a framework for ideals which are inspiring and sustaining to our life.

We invest our deities with the most illustrious attributes we desire to possess, and then through the emulation of these attributes, we make something of ourselves: as human beings and as spiritual beings. The humanity in us is in the making by mirroring in our lives the qualities we vested in our deities. This is a supreme and salutary aspect of traditional religions.

A MAN WITHOUT RELIGION IS LIKE A HORSE WITHOUT A BRIDLE.

Latin Proverb

RELIGION AIDS IN SEARCH FOR IDENTITY

Religion in the ultimate analysis is an instrument in man's search for his identity, his integrity, his painful struggles with himself to attain and preserve humanity. Life has created an arsenal of means and devices to enhance and perpetuate itself. On the level of human consciousness and human culture, it has created art and religion as the instruments for safeguarding its highest accomplishments. Take, for example, language. It is a human invention, a means of human communication. But seen in a broader perspective, language is an instrument of life articulating itself.

REFINEMENT OF LIFE

One of the partial conclusions then is: do not be overly impressed by the secondary aspects of religion, art or language: specifically, do not narrow your attention to their pathological aspects, but look at them as the vehicles of articulation and refinement of life at large: and then you will be closer to being a son of heaven.

When conceived as instruments of perfectibility of man, worship and religion have positive functions. However, infatuated with the ideal of material progress, we have forgotten about those salutary aspects of traditional religions. Euripides had it right when he said:

Who rightly with necessity complies
In things divine we count him skilled and wise.

Modern thinkers, such as Nietzsche, Marx, Engels, the Marxists and so many humanists of various denominations of our times have got it wrong about religion. For they have concentrated on its secondary functions and its negative functions. While denying religion, they so often have negated the spiritual heritage of mankind. In fighting against the last vestiges of traditional religion, Christianity in particular, they have inadvertently shrunk the meaning of man's existence by reducing it to man's economic activity.

WE NEED RELIGION

Religion offers the simplest, clearest, and easiest approach to the recognition of nature and reality. It is spiritual understanding that is ultimately meaningful, ultimately profitable to our wellbeing and wholeness—no investigation into the world of materiality can substitute for it.

The Christian Science Monitor, February 4, 1977

Even if we are unable to prove that culture and religion are attributes of life unfolding, it would be worthwhile to believe that this is so. And who of us with certainty is going to prove that this is not so? And why would anybody like to prove that, namely, to prove the unprovable?

"Religion has kept the world 10,000 years behind time."

Religion Is a Gigantic Fraud

James Hervey Johnson

James Hervey Johnson is one of the leading voices of organized atheism in America today. The bulk of his writings (including his book, *The Case Against Religion*) amounts to a sustained attack upon religion in general and Christianity in particular. In the following viewpoint, Johnson attempts to show why "Religion Is a Gigantic Fraud."

Consider the following questions while reading:

1. If religion is a fraud, why, according to Johnson, is it "kept alive?"
2. Why does the author believe that the "goodness of God is a fraud?'"
3. Do you agree or disagree with the author? Why or why not?

James Hervey Johnson, *Religion Is a Gigantic Fraud.* Reprinted with permission of the author and through the courtesy of The Truth Seeker Co., Inc., Box 2832, San Diego CA 92112.

Intelligent men do not form a conclusion until they have carefully studied both, or even more sides of a subject. Fools do not make such an examination but accept blindly any dogmas or doctrines imposed upon them, often when they were children, by priests, clergy or others. As children, they were unable to reason.

RELIGION BASED ON SUPERSTITION

Those who have examined the facts find that religion is a gigantic fraud, based upon the superstitious beliefs of ignorant primitive barbarians. They find that religion is kept alive because it is immensely profitable to the people who promote it. In the U.S., churches own 80 billion dollars worth of property and have more than ten billion dollars annual income, all tax exempt. The clergy are exempt from the harshness and risk of death and injury in war, and they have many other privileges such as half fare or less on planes, buses and trains. So they do all they can to keep their deceptive superstitions alive.

The clergy are trained for years to be deceivers. They start with the 4 year olds. They are taught to twist meanings so as to make people think black is white. Their other principal activity is to extract money from their victims. They even collect pennies from the little children in Sunday School, to get them in the habit of giving money to the Church.

HEALERS OF SOULS

The church is a sort of hospital for men's souls, and as full of quackery as the hospital for their bodies.

Henry David Thoreau, *The Christian Fable*

Science has proven that there is no God, no heaven, no hell, no devil, no angels, no witches (although the Bible says they should be killed). Common sense tells us that the Christian doctrine of turning the other cheek to enemies only puts good men at the mercy of evil ones. Science proves the universe operates according to natural law.

The facts are that religion has caused and still causes untold misery, unhappiness, wars and trouble. Religion has kept the world 10,000 years behind time.

We do not ask or expect you to take our word for this. We only ask you to make your own investigation. We ask you to study what great scientists and scholars have proven to be true, much of which evidence is available in their writings. So powerful is the greed of

"I ALREADY KNOW THE WORD OF GOD. DAD SAYS GOD'S FAVORITE WORD IS *MONEY!*"

the clergy, however, that they have been successful in preventing such material from being found in most public libraries, in colleges, or in the press, radio and TV programs.

Those who have a spark of intelligence will investigate. The dumb will continue to be exploited by the deceiving clergy. Some unfortunates have been bred, for centuries, like sheep, to be gullible believers. The churches have killed or imprisoned the thinkers, (like Galileo, Bruno and Servetus murdered and tortured because they said the world was round and not the center of the universe) ostracized, smeared, libelled and slandered them, so the dumb believers are in the majority. They are unable to reason.

GOD'S GOODNESS IS A FRAUD

Any one can prove that the so called goodness of God is a fraud. Every day there are earthquakes, hurricanes, and other disasters that a good god could prevent if there was one. A good god would not permit little children to die of cancer, nor allow them to be born blind, deformed, deaf, and suffer from polio and syphilis. A decent god would not make tapeworms, lice, fleas, chiggers, diseased brains, idiots and insanity.

Prove to yourself that prayers are worthless. Preachers pray in a loud voice to impress their sheep. Even their imaginary God, Jesus, said they should pray in secret and that those who prayed aloud were hypocrites.(Mat. 6:5)

"Churches are teachers. They transmit meanings for life and the values that people have found essential for their fulfillment."

Churches Are Helpful Teachers

Andrew Panzarella

Andrew Panzarella is a member of The Brothers of the Christian Schools. A practicing psychologist, he has taught at the high school and college levels since 1963. In his book, *Religion and Human Experience,* Andrew Panzarella combines his experiences as a religious and a psychologist "to emphasize how individual each person is and how different religion can be for each person." The following viewpoint is an excerpt from that book.

Consider the following questions while reading:
1. **Why does the author claim churches are teachers?**
2. **In what ways do churches "offer advantages in terms of political and economic power?"**
3. **According to Panzarella, how do the churches of today differ from those of an earlier period?**

Andrew Panzarella, *Religion and Human Experience.* Saint Mary's College Press, Winona, Minnesota, Copyright 1974.

Many persons are content to be religious without belonging to churches—maybe because of a strong personal need for religious individuality, or maybe because they were brought up outside church structures and never felt a need for them, or maybe because they once belonged to a church and found no significant benefit in membership. They seem to be no less good or fulfilled than church members. Still, there are advantages in religious organization which these people may experience in other kinds of groups or in less formal ways.

CHURCHES ARE TEACHERS

Perhaps the most important advantage in church membership is the sharing of values and meaning. Churches are teachers. They transmit meanings for life and the values that people have found essential for their fulfillment. Not only do the churches frequently take the task of introducing meanings and values to the young if parents fail to do so, but they also continue to reinforce these meanings and values throughout the entire lifespan of the individual.

As teachers, the churches should also help the individual to continually reassess the meanings and values that are transmitted. Within the church as a group will be found perceptive and thought-provoking members who help the others to shed inadequate notions and to grow continuously. Thus the church member may find if easier than the non-church-member to get beyond the religion of childhood to a mature religious orientation.

CHURCHES PROMOTE NECESSARY CHANGES

Churches also offer advantages in terms of political and economic power. Undeniably this power has been, and sometimes still is, used by churches to force themselves or their distinct values on a society. Nearly everyone can find some causes he disagrees with. The person who objects to Catholic power in Spain or Protestant power in Northern Ireland might be in favor of the involvement of some of the U.S. churches in civil rights or in welfare legislation. Unless a person uses religion as an escape from responsibility by cultivating a leave-it-to-God attitude, he is bound to be concerned about the injustices within a society. The concerned individual, however, is relatively impotent compared to an organized group of concerned people.

Not too long ago there appeared in the *New York Times* a full-page advertisement paid for by laymen of various churches protesting the involvement of their denominations in social issues. They were calling for the churches to rid themselves of all interests other than preaching the word of God. In the past churches have always done more than preach. Institutions like schools, hospitals, and orphanages were originally nurtured primarily by churches and only later taken over by public, secular agencies. Churches often seem to be bolder than governments in undertaking new social enterprises. Even if one argues that churches should back out of social areas once adequate secular systems have been developed, the churches would still be engaged in social issues, for it is their particular penchant frequently to spot a society's needs and weaknesses before the society as a whole is ready to do anything about them.

The Western churches of today function in society precisely opposite to the way the churches of the medieval and early modern period moved. In the Middle Ages and in the centuries immediately following the Reformation, the churches were the stabilizing and homogenizing forces in society. They were closely allied with governments and preserved the *status quo*. They discouraged change. As a matter of fact, the churches continued to favor the old monarchical governments even after the people overthrew them. Nowadays the churches see themselves more as critics and agitators whose function is to encourage the changes that seem necessary in society. Thus it is to society as well as to individuals that churches offer advantages.

DISTINGUISHING BETWEEN STATEMENTS THAT ARE PROVABLE AND THOSE THAT ARE NOT

From various sources of information we are constantly confronted with statements and generalizations about social and moral problems. In order to think clearly about these problems, it is useful if one can make a basic distinction between statements which cannot be verified because evidence is not available, or the issue is so controversial that it cannot be definitely proved. Students constantly should be aware that textbooks, newspaper editorials and magazine articles often contain statements of a controversial nature. The following activity is designed to allow you to critically evaluate statements that are provable and those that are not. Some of them have been taken from viewpoints in this book.

In each of the following statements indicate whether you believe it is provable (P), too controversial to be proved to everyone's satisfaction (C), or unprovable because of the lack of evidence (U). Compare and discuss your results with your classmates.

P = Provable
C = Too Controversial
U = Unprovable

_____ 1. Belief in God is the best way we know for relating to the mystery and the paradox that lie at the very heart of life.

_____ 2. Most of us are taught that when we die our soul survives.

_____ 3. When we die, our soul survives.

_____ 4. Jesus Christ came not to destroy the law or the prophets but to fulfill that which was prophesied.

_____ 5. Scientists have not been able to demonstrate the "first cause" therefore God must be the "First Cause."

_____ 6. The belief in an eternal God provides comfort and meaning in the lives of many people.

_____ 7. Women cannot be ordained ministers because Jesus Christ, as revealed to us in the Bible, did not approve of it.

_____ 8. When feminists succeed in changing the position of women in Christianity and Judaism, the very foundations of these religions will be radically altered.

_____ 9. When women are given access to positions of authority in all Christian Churches, Christianity will increase in stature and prestige in the eyes of the non-Christian world.

_____ 10. Even the skeptical historian develops a humble respect for religion, since he sees if functioning and seemingly indispensable in every land and age.

_____ 11. A religious person is, by necessity, dependent and other-directed rather than independent and self-directed.

_____ 12. In the name of God, many atrocities have been committed by people against other people throughout history.

_____ 13. Religion is slavery.

BIBLIOGRAPHY OF PERIODICAL ARTICLES

Glenn R. Bucher — *Liberation Theology,* **Intellect,** February, 1977, p. 278.

Jeff Calkins — *Organized Religion: Who Needs It?,* **Plain Truth,** May, 1977, p. 20.

John Cogley — *The Gods Keep Failing,* **The Center Magazine,** March/April 1974, p. 2.

Jeffrey Hart — *Morality Is Based on Religion,* **Human Events,** February 5, 1977, p. 15.

Abraham Joshua Heschel — *The Abiding Challenge of Religion,* **The Center Magazine,** March/April 1973, p. 43.

George Jacob Holyoake — *Listen to Humanity Rather than Bigotry,* **The Humanist,** November/December 1975, p. 48.

Marvin Kohl and Joseph Fletcher — *Morality Without Religion,* **Free Inquiry,** Winter 1980/1981, p. 28.

Konstantin Kolenda — *Humanism and Christianity,* **The Humanist,** July/August, 1980.

Ernest Morgan — *Do We Need Christianity?,* **The Humanist,** March/April, 1980, p. 43.

John Platt — *World Transformation: Changes in Belief Systems,* **The Futurist,** June, 1974, p. 124.

Ignatz Sahula-Dyke — *Want To Be Governed by Clerics?,* **The American Atheist,** December, 1980, p. 15.

Warren Shibles — *Catholicism: A World Political Movement,* **The American Atheist,** March, 1977, p. 22.

Andrew E. Slaby, Peter J. Fagan and Laurence R. Tancredi — *A Second Look at Religion and Freudianism,* **America,** May 19, 1976, p. 469.

Bob G. Slosser — *In Defense of the Organized Church,* **National Courier,** April 1, 1977.

Time — *Saints Among Us,* December 29, 1975, p. 47.

Arnold Toynbee — *Is Religion Superfluous?,* **Intellectual Digest,** December, 1971, p. 58.

Dwayne Walls — *The Jesus Mania: Bigotry in the Name of the Lord,* **Saturday Review,** September 17, 1977, p. 13.

APPENDIX OF PUBLICATIONS

The following publications are essentially religious in nature. However, in addition to presenting a wide range of articles and editorials on religion, many of the publications also contain secular news of national and international interest.

America
106 West 56th Street
New York, NY 10019

Published weekly by the Jesuits of the U.S. and Canada, a Roman Catholic religious order. $18.00 per year

The Christian Century
407 South Dearborn Street
Chicago, IL 60605

Published weekly by the Christian Century Foundation. The magazine has a liberal Protestant point of view. $18.00 per year

Christianity Today
465 Gundersen Drive
Carol Stream, IL 60187

Published Semi-Monthly. This magazine has an evangelical christian point of view. $21.00 per year

Christianity and Crisis
Subscription Department
P.O. Box 1308-C
Fort Lee, NJ 07024

Published bi-weekly. This magazine has a liberal christian point of view. $15.00 per year

Commentary
165 East 56th Street
New York, NY 10022

Published monthly by the American Jewish Committee. $27.00 per year

Commonweal
232 Madison Avenue
New York, NY 10016

Published bi-weekly. This magazine has a liberal Roman Catholic point of view. $22.00 per year

Eternity
1716 Spruce Street
Philadelphia, PA 19103

Published monthly by Evangelical Ministries, a christian organization. $14.00 per year

Liberty
6840 Eastern Avenue NW
Washington, DC 20012

Published bi-monthly by the Religious Liberty Association of America and the Seventh-day Adventist Church. No charge

Moment
P.O. Box 922
Farmingdale, NY 11733

Published monthly by Jewish Educational Ventures.
$22.00 per year

Moody Monthly
2101 West Howard Street
Chicago, IL 60645

Published monthly by the Moody Bible Institute. It is a member of the Evangelical Press Association, a christian organization.
$12.95 per year

Present Tense
111 8th Avenue
New York, NY 10011

Published quarterly by the American Jewish Committee and deals with world Jewish affairs. $12.00 per year

Sojourners
1309 L Street NW
Washington, DC 20005

Published monthly. This magazine has a liberal christian point of view.
$12.00 per year

U.S. Catholic
221 West Madison Street
Chicago, IL 60606

Published monthly by the Claretian Fathers and Brothers, a Roman Catholic religious order. $12.00 per year

The following publications are humanistic or overtly anti-religious. The editors wish to note that magazines of this nature are extremely scarce.

American Atheist
P.O. Box 2117
Austin, Texas 78768

Published monthly by the American Atheists.
$25.00 per year

Free Inquiry
Box 5, Central Park Station
Buffalo, NY 14215

Published quarterly by the Council for Democratic and Secular Humanism.
$12.00 per year

The Humanist
7 Harwood Drive
Amherst, NY 14226

Published bi-monthly by the American Humanist Association.
$12.00 per year

Index

MEET THE EDITORS

David L. Bender is a history graduate from the University of Minnesota. He also has a M.A. in government from St. Mary's University in San Antonio, Texas. He has taught social problems at the high school level for several years. He is the general editor of the Opposing Viewpoints Series and has authored most of the titles in the series.

Bruno Leone received his B.A. (Phi Kappa Phi) from Arizona State University and his M.A. in history from the University of Minnesota. A Woodrow Wilson Fellow (1967), he is currently an instructor at Minneapolis Community College, Minne-apolis, Minnesota, where he has taught history, anthropology, and political science. In 1974-75, he was awarded a Fellowship by the National Endowment for the Humanities to research the intellectual origins of American Democracy.